T0266662

For the Love of Jeremy

For the Love of Jeremy

A Memoir of a Family Affliction: Mental Health and Addiction

Renate LeDuc

GREEN PLACE BOOKS *Brattleboro, Vermont*

All of the stories in this book are true based on the author's memory and journal entries. The conversations all come from recollections, although they are not written to represent word for word transcripts but retold in a way that incites the feeling and meaning of what was said. The essence of the dialogue is accurate.

Names, identifying details, and geographical locations have been altered or omitted to protect the privacy and integrity of all involved.

Printed in the United States.

10 9 8 7 6 5 4 3 2 1

Green Writers Press is a Vermont-based publisher whose mission is to spread a message of hope and renewal through the words and images we publish. Throughout we will adhere to our commitment to preserving and protecting the natural resources of the earth. To that end, a percentage of our proceeds will be donated to environmental activist groups and social justice organizations. Green Writers Press gratefully acknowledges support from individual donors, friends, and readers to help support the environment and our publishing initiative. Green Place Books curates books that tell literary and compelling stories with a focus on writing about place—these books are more personal stories, memoir, and biographies.

GREEN PLACE BOOKS

green writers press

Giving Voice to Writers & Artists Who Will Make the World a Better Place
Green Writers Press | Brattleboro, Vermont
www.greenwriterspress.com

ISBN: 979-8-9865324-4-8

FRONTISPIECE ARTWORK: *Jaehnel LeDuc Gulick*

PRINTED ON PAPER WITH PULP THAT COMES FROM FSC-CERTIFIED FORESTS, MANAGED FORESTS THAT GUARANTEE RESPONSIBLE ENVIRONMENTAL, SOCIAL, AND ECONOMIC PRACTICES.

For the love of Jeremy

Our lives are stories, and the stories we have to give to each other are the most important. No one has a story too small and all are of equal stature. We each tell them in different ways, through different mediums—and if we care about each other, we'll take the time to listen.

—CHARLES DE LINT

Contents

A Note to Readers

SINCE SOME TIME HAS PASSED between the original writing and the publishing of this book, times have changed and less stigmatizing language is evolving surrounding addiction and mental illness:

"Fentanyl poisoning" is preferred over the use of "overdose" when fentanyl is a factor in toxicology. This is due to the fact that miniscule amounts of fentanyl (the size of 2 salt granules) can be and often are fatal. Most victims are deceived and unaware that fentanyl is in the contents of what they are taking. Thus, "poisoning" is considered a more appropriate term.

Substance Use Disorder and Substance User are preferred terms over Addiction and Addict since it indicates more of a disease model than a moral failing.

There are also advocates hoping to change the term "mental illness" to "brain disorder" or "brain disease" since it truly is a manifestation of a physical condition in the body.

Of course, changes take time, especially when terms are nationally accepted and used for decades.

For the Love of Jeremy

April 1999

Easter week in 1999, Jeremy came home from his school in Rhode Island for a week vacation. A couple of days after his arrival, Jeremy's friend Mark was riding home from a party with his girlfriend, Sarah, who was driving. They had a head-on collision with another boy that was at the same party.

Sarah was in a coma, and Mark was in bad shape, with broken bones and his mouth wired shut. As Jeremy was leaving to drive back to school, he stopped at the hospital to visit. Mark was distraught and told Jeremy that they were disconnecting Sarah's life support. They did, and Sarah died later that day.

This visit left such an impact on Jeremy. He was truly an empath with so much compassion for others. A few days later, we received a phone call from the administration at his school. They were worried about Jeremy because he had not yet shown up for school and hadn't called. This was so unlike him. The school knew he had bipolar disorder. An hour later I received a call from a New Hampshire police officer. He asked me if I knew Jeremy LeDuc. I said yes, that I was his mother.

"His mother? He said his mother was dead," the officer replied. Mark's mother had died a few years before, from cancer.

The officer continued. "He said he was in a head-on collision and his girlfriend died. He can't seem to explain where the car is, though. We found him wandering around in an abandoned lot in his bare feet. He had grass in his pockets and said it was making him high."

"Oh, my God, he thinks he's his friend Mark," I said. He had put himself in his friend's place and couldn't tell the difference between what was real and what wasn't. He must have stopped taking his medication, I realized. I told the officer that we would leave to get there right away but it would take us at least seven hours. The officer said he didn't think he could get Jeremy to stay; he was pacing and wanted to leave. The officer was very kind when I told him that Jeremy had bipolar and that he must have stopped taking his medication—and that the death and accident of his friends must have thrown him into an episode.

The officer offered a solution. He said he would arrest Jeremy for trespassing and put him in a jail cell to ensure that he would still be there when we got there. Then he would drop the charges on Monday. The date was April 9, 1999, exactly four years after Jeremy's original diagnosis and hospitalization.

Bob and I left New Jersey about 8:00 P.M. and got to New Hampshire at about three in the morning. When we got there, the officers said they had been watching Jeremy in the cell on the TV screen, and he was taking off his pants and shirt and ripping his jeans in pieces with his bare hands. We watched on the screen for a few minutes. It was so sad; so unfair.

They let Jeremy out of the cell and he hugged us and cried when he saw us. We had brought clothes and helped him get dressed. He said he was on his way to work Wednesday and got lost.

He hadn't had his medicine with him. His ATM card showed that he had driven to Massachusetts, down to Connecticut, and back up to New Hampshire. He had been driving for two days straight with no sleep. The police had found his car on the side of the road and it had been towed.

We went to get Jeremy's car out of the impound lot. It would have been nice to go to a hotel and get some sleep, but there was no way that Jeremy would sleep. He was manic and not at all tired, so we stopped at Jeremy's apartment for clothes and his medicine and drove back to New Jersey. I drove my car and Bob drove Jeremy's car with Jeremy in the passenger seat. We were so tired. Jeremy was completely delusional and kept insisting they couldn't put the radio on because people were after him and contacting him through the radio.

When we got home around noon the next day, Bob and I took turns sleeping. Jeremy was so irrational that we could not leave him alone. He went around the house unplugging all the plugs so that "they couldn't contact him." He picked up all the mail and papers with our names on them in the house and shredded them. He picked at his forehead until there was an open wound. He said that "they" had planted a chip in his forehead to track him.

We talked to Jeremy's psychiatrist, who doubled his medication and added something to help him sleep. He finally fell asleep on the sofa. It was four days since he went missing and who knows how many days prior that he hadn't slept. I looked at him. My beautiful boy. I gently put my hand through his sandy-colored, wavy hair and kissed him on the forehead and said I was so sorry. I went to step away and he picked up his head and hugged me hard. I saw his blue-green eyes connect with mine and I was so relieved. In that moment, I felt my Jeremy still in there.

Coming to America

43 YEARS EARLIER

THE BEST PART was swirling the chocolate into the creamy batter in the bundt pans. I was only three years old, and I loved baking the marble cakes with Mutti. Mutti smiled at my delight. This is the only time I remember my Mutti smiling.

"Mutti, why does Oma cry so much"? I had seen Oma trying to shield her tears several times during the past few months and didn't understand why. She lived upstairs in our home so we saw her often, and went freely up and down the stairs to visit.

"Oh, little Renate, she is sad because we are moving to America."

"Is America very far away?"

"Yes, I'm afraid so. It may be a long time before we see Oma and Opa Beckman, all your Onkels und Tantes and your cousins again."

"Why do we have to go?"

"Oh, my Liebchen, your Papa has worked very hard to get approval for our family to go to America. We have waited a long time for this. He feels we will have a better life in America and he will feel safer there. There are reasons he does not feel safe with us living so close to East Germany after the war."

"I don't want to go. What will happen to Oma? She is getting old. Who will take care of her? What will happen to our house? Papa built it for us."

"Papa is giving our house to Tante Erika and Onkel Karl Heinz, and Oma will continue to live upstairs. They will take good care of her."

I knew she was trying to reassure me, but I couldn't help noticing the tears in her eyes ready to overflow. Of course, at only three years old, I didn't know how far America actually was. I didn't know that I would not see my relatives for years, and that I may never see Oma again.

It was a long plane ride through the night, then a boat bringing us somewhere. It couldn't have been Ellis Island, because it had closed two years before, but I remember the cheers on the boat when we saw the Statue of Liberty. The cheerfulness quickly turned to fear as so many immigrants were lined up in white medical gowns. We were waiting to be examined by doctors. Even as a three-year-old, I felt "less than;" like cattle.

Then our new American Family emerged and we were introduced. They had sponsored us through the Lutheran Church. Helen Kirsch was a plump, jovial woman. She approached us with big bear hugs and a German/English dictionary in hand. By her side was her graying and handsome husband, Walter, and his warm smile. Behind them stood Walter's brother, Fred, and his wife, Mary. Mary was thin with short, gray hair and Fred was balding but also very handsome. Their eyes and smiles clearly showed the kindness of all four of them.

The Kirsch's didn't speak German, and we didn't speak English, but somehow we managed with German/English dictionaries. They brought us to our new home that they had secured for us. It was a three-bedroom upstairs apartment in a two-family home with the outside shingles so weathered that they appeared black. The apartment was roomy, clean, and furnished. My sister Christa and I were to share a bedroom. My half-sister, Ruth, thirteen years old, had another bedroom, and my parents had the third bedroom. Our landlord was a man we hardly ever saw. He was about a hundred years old and our rent was a hundred dollars a month. Our American Family had secured a job for my father making—yes—a hundred dollars a week!

My father did autobody work for a shop called Englehardt Brothers in Hackensack, New Jersey. My father had trained in autobody work in Germany and had worked for Volkswagen there. Of course, my father didn't yet have a driver's license or a car, but we lived in Maywood, which was only a fifteen-minute bus ride to Hackensack.

My sisters were placed a year behind in school so they would have time to learn the English language. Since I had a year and a half before I started kindergarten, I had the benefit of learning English before I started school. My parents went to citizenship classes right away. They had to learn the English language and American history. They both passed the test, but there was still a required waiting time to become a citizen.

It was easier for my father because he was out in the world working. I'm sure my mother started to feel very isolated without her relatives and with difficulty communicating with neighbors and acquaintances. Even though they had passed the test, German would remain the language they were more comfortable with, and their English remained broken. My mother's heart also broke and remained broken. She felt the loss, every day, of her mother and father as well as the rest of her family. My sisters and I had school and began to make friends, but our Mutti had no friends, and not knowing the language, didn't know how to make them.

Christmas Eve came only eight days after we arrived in America. My family walked the two blocks to Two Guys that day, and my father excitedly led us around the store asking us what we would want Kris Kringle to bring us. I wondered if Kris Kringle shopped at Two Guys. We went home and put up our Christmas tree. It was always the German tradition not to decorate the tree until Christmas Eve.

When the tree was all decorated, Papa told Christa and me to play in the bedroom. A few minutes later, Papa came in and shouted, "Come see! Kris Kringle came!" We ran out, and sure enough, there were all the gifts we had picked out at Two Guys: the electric organ, transistor radio, jewelry box, and more. Even at three, I was too smart to believe that Kris Kringle happened to bring everything we had just picked out at Two Guys. That was the beginning of the end of a childhood that included Santa Claus for me!

Our home was only one block from the main street of Maywood . It had a butcher shop, bakery, candy store, and really any other shop you might need. My sister Christa and I walked to the shops almost every day. We took turns picking up fresh rye bread at the bakery. It was thirty-seven cents a loaf. We used to fight over the ends of the bread. We both loved the hard, crusty outside and the fresh soft inside. The ends of the bread were called the *Kanuse* in German. To this day, I still grab for the *Kanuse* when we get fresh rye bread.

We used to love to go to the bakery. The lady behind the counter would always offer us a free cookie. The scent of buttery baked goods and all the delectable delights in the window were tantalizing! Occasionally, we would add a crumb cake to our order. Christa and I would eat crumbs off the cake, which were the best part. One day we couldn't help ourselves and ate all the crumbs off of the crumb cake. My Papa was so angry. For punishment he made us eat the whole cake with no crumbs on it. I can think of worse punishments, but we did each have a stomachache.

Another store we would frequent was the butcher's. I loved the aroma of the hanging meats. The butcher always gave me a piece of the fresh bologna when he sliced it. He was so jolly and sang while he was preparing meats for his loyal customers. I also loved the smell of the shoemaker shop. My parents always had the soles on their shoes repaired. I would bring their shoes there and pick them up. The smell of the leather was euphoric. Then there was the candy shop. All the candy bars were a nickel and there was even a bunch of penny candy. We definitely loved to go there every day. That probably had a lot to do with the fact that when I went to the dentist for the first time in second grade, I had eleven cavities.

There was also a pet shop on Main Street that we would often frequent to see all the different animals. Once there were a dozen baby chicks and they were so cute. My sister and I decided to bring them home to our apartment. We tried to hide them for a while from my Papa, but then he found them in our bedroom and oh boy, was he upset. He yelled, "We can't keep them! They grow up to be chickens. They belong on a farm." Christa and I enjoyed playing with them while they were cute little chicks. We had them in a cardboard box and used to let them practice diving into the box from the palm of our hands. Then my father found a farm that would take them. We were sorry to see them go, but I guess we knew it was for the best.

Another time, we brought home a kitten from the pet shop. He said what he always did: *Mensch das Kinder noch mal.* In German this meant, "Man, those kids again!" The kitten grew to be a cat and one night my father woke us in the middle of the night and said, "Come out here! I want you to see something." We wandered out to the dining room, half asleep.

There, in our birdcage, were two dead parakeets. He said, "See what you did? I told you you shouldn't have brought that cat home!" We felt terrible. After that, we tried not to bring pets home without permission.

Looking back, I realize my parents really let us experience adventures. We weren't afraid of my parents, even though we caused my father a lot of frustration and aggravation. Mutti was always a quiet bystander in my memory.

I didn't realize until I was older how lost we would have been without the Kirsches, our American Family. They had found us a place to live within walking distance to everything we needed, *and* a job for my father. Of course, I also learned later on that these sponsorships were requirements for immigration at the time. So here we were, our family of five, in a new country, with a new language, new culture, and the fear of the unknown.

Ruth: The Beginning of Her Madness

My oldest sister, Ruth (well, she was really my half-sister from my mother's first marriage), was old enough to babysit at sixteen, so my mother got a factory job. It was summer and we were all home from school. Christa and I had many friends in the neighborhood and we were always out playing with them.

My sister Ruth was an attractive, mature-looking teen. She had pretty brunette hair and a great figure. Sometimes, when we stopped home, there was a strange man there with Ruth. In fact, he was our garbage man. I knew that garbage men didn't come in the house to pick up garbage, so I wondered if she went outside to meet him and invited him in. He often had his arms around her, and he always offered us a quarter if we would go to the corner store, buy ice cream, and stay away for two hours. Of course, we were asked to keep it a secret. We reluctantly obliged, even though there was something scary about it. I suppose that's why we never told our parents.

Several months later, Ruth went missing for two days. My parents were frantic. They called the police. They really didn't know who else to call. Ruth didn't have friends, and they had no idea where to look for her. Then, one early evening, she showed up at home and announced she was leaving to live with her new boyfriend. She started packing her bags. My father was yelling at her, saying, "Where have you been and where do you think you're going?" He was pulling her arm, telling her she was not leaving. She was thrashing and pulling with resistance and was obviously not going to stay home. My father must have called the police, because they soon came and took both her and her boyfriend away. Her boyfriend looked like an old man to me, at least three or four times her age. I asked Papa where the police were taking them. He said they were taking her boyfriend to jail and Ruth to the hospital to be evaluated.

A couple of days later, we visited Ruth at Bergen Pines, which is now known as Bergen Community Hospital. I was too young to be allowed in, so I waved to Ruth through the window. The window had bars on it. She looked so sad. That picture has stayed in my mind, always.

This was yet another traumatic event for Mutti. She could no longer work because we no longer had Ruth as a babysitter. When I think about what few memories I have of her, I realize this was around the time she was always on the sofa. In the morning, after school, at night, there she was, deep in despair. We had TV dinners for dinner, which Christa and I thought were great. Papa had to take over much of managing the household, even though he worked six days a week.

I thought Ruth would come home soon, but she never did. Before long, we were visiting her every Sunday at a place for troubled girls called St. Mary's in upstate New York. My father didn't have a driver's license or a car yet, so the Kirsches drove the long ride with us each week. I wonder if they wished they had sponsored a different immigrant family. I'm sure we were more than they bargained for. Despite this, they never complained and were always there for us, ready to help.

I enjoyed the Sunday visits because we always went out to dinner on the way home and really, my family never went out to dinner. These were the wonderful dinners where I first tasted French fries, London broil, and strawberry shortcake.

Ruth actually seemed quite happy at St. Mary's. She had a beautiful voice and sang solos in all the shows there. She was stunning, and the other girls looked up to her. Here, she fit in. In High School in Maywood, I don't remember her having one friend. She hated school. But here she was, in her element. Here with all the girls that were different, that didn't fit in at home. Ruth stayed at St. Mary's for two years, until she graduated high school.

My Mother's Madness

Some may have described the home we lived in as a charcoal gray, but to me as a seven-year-old, it was black. I was in second grade, and every house I drew I would color in black crayon.

One day, my teacher got fed up and picked up my picture and showed it to the class. "Why in the world would you always color a house black? How many black houses have you seen?"

A boy raised his hand. "Well, Renate's house is black. And her mother walks around and around the block talking to herself and she spits on the sidewalk."

The teacher looked like she saw a ghost and handed my picture back to me. This may have been the first time I realized our life was not normal. No one else's family was like mine.

When I was eight years old, Papa got his driver's license and bought a car, a shiny black Falcon. It was a damaged car at the shop where he worked and he fixed it up himself after work and on weekends. He bought it for—you guessed it—a hundred dollars!

This development would change our lives. Papa was now no longer limited to living where he could catch the bus to work. He had always loved the country, so on weekends we started taking drives out to the countryside looking for homes to buy. Englehart Brothers, where Papa worked, was opening a shop in Hawthorne, New Jersey, so it was planned that we would move to a location near there. My parents settled for a little two-bedroom house in Oakland, New Jersey for $12,000. It was 1963.

Ruth had already graduated high school at St. Mary's and was attending Dover Business College, renting a room near the school. She lived in Englewood, which was about twenty minutes away from our old house in Maywood and thirty minutes away from our new house in Oakland. Despite the close distance, I never remember visiting her.

Christa and I were so angry that we were moving. Christa and I were inseparable, and we had built a strong comradery with the neighborhood kids. Our neighborhood antics resembled that of *The Little Rascals* and we feared the fun we had would never be the same, living in the country in the middle of nowhere! But Christa and I adjusted quickly, making new friends in the neighborhood and in school. You just don't know how much you're going to like something until you try it.

I wish I could say our Mutti acclimated as well. We soon learned that the last thing that Mutti needed at the time was another major change. Still not driving or speaking English very well at all, she quickly became isolated at home. At least in Maywood, she could walk to several shops a block away. Our home soon became a showcase of her instability. There was so much clutter and disarray.

One day shortly after we moved to Oakland, we were all home. Christa and I had gone to school that day and my father had come home from work the usual time, about 6 o'clock. There was no dinner cooking. We were all in the living room. My father took both Mutti's hands and looked at her wrists. He started to cry and say, "Why, why? Why are you doing this?" I looked at her wrists and saw deep cuts. I didn't understand what was happening and I didn't ask. I was afraid to. A few weeks later, I woke up to a shrill scream. I was in a complete state of confusion, not understanding what was happening. My sister crying uncontrollably as she ran into the bedroom we shared. She had woken up early to shower and get dressed for work. Her screams woke Papa as well. Papa was opening the bathroom door wondering why the weight of the door was so heavy. Then Papa was crying. I'd only once seen him cry, and not like this. It sounded almost like a howling. He kept saying "Why, why?"

Before I knew it, our pastor was sitting on the side of our bed. Christa and I cried while he prayed. I don't think anyone actually told me what happened, but they didn't have to. I knew, even though I was in shock and it didn't seem real. I was ten and Christa was thirteen. I could only imagine how vivid the picture was in the minds of my sister and Papa. My mother was only forty-three. So young—but maybe more at peace. The voices were quieted. The suffering was over.

If trauma is a trigger for bipolar disorder, I can't imagine much worse trauma than learning that your child, that Ruth, had the same mental illness that had been haunting you for years—and then being completely isolated, having no one to talk to about it. At that time, it was called manic-depressive illness, but not very often, because no one talked about it. I lost my mother, but truly, I had already lost her years before. She had been emotionally absent throughout most of the previous four or five years. I knew that other mothers were different but I believe children usually accept their family dynamics the way they are without questioning.

At the time, I didn't know anyone who had experienced this in their family. I couldn't find the words to explain it to anyone. Years later, when I read the memoir of Victoria Rowell, who was raised in foster care due to her mother's mental illness, I came across these words:

> —how would I explain? I could no more ignore my mother's illness than I could reciprocate her odd affection. My dispassion concerned me as much as my helpless wish to rescue her from something I had no comprehension of. The shift in my thinking was the solid knowledge that I was not my mother but I loved her and grieved for her. I could find compassion for her without blaming myself for not being a better daughter. (Victoria Rowell 2008)

In March of 1963, my mother decided she could no longer live on this earth with the rest of us. I once read that people who die of suicide truly believe that their loved ones are better off without them. I guess as a child I thought she didn't love me and my sisters enough to stay. My first reaction was shock, along with denial. My mind could not accept what had just happened. I thought it was a nightmare and that I would soon wake up. My thoughts were disoriented.

My sister and I spent the next two days at the funeral home for the wake. It was an open casket. I had never been to a wake or a funeral before. The shock served to protect me for a few days so I could manage to participate in the funeral services. Friends and neighbors came, but all of our relatives were in Germany. Friends and neighbors reached out to us with cards and flowers. They brought us food, and offered babysitting for me when my sister had after-school activities. Their condolences were comforting.

Ruth came home. She hadn't lived with us since she had been hospitalized and went away to school. Every time I had seen her the past three years, she seemed relatively stable. I was glad she was coming home. I looked up to her. She was beautiful and talented. She could sing, play the accordion, and sew beautifully. But I became concerned when I saw Ruth's grief so controlled. I remember hoping she would cry, and feeling relieved when she finally did. I suppose I needed the assurance that she was grieving.

In the days that followed, I was under control during the day but I cried every night when I went to bed. I felt sadness that my mother was in so much pain that she had to end her life. I also felt guilt. I remembered a few days before she died, she had hugged me and told me that she loved me and asked if I loved her. That picture kept coming back to me. I thought if I had given her a stronger hug or had been more convincing, maybe she would have changed her mind. I know she wanted me to know she loved me, and that what she was about to do was not my fault. Because of my age, I probably felt less guilt than my father, who must have felt a tremendous amount of guilt. No one mentioned my mother's death when I went back to school after a few days. No counseling was recommended. There was an article in the paper that included the detail that our mother had hung herself. I'm not sure who, exactly, but some friends or acquaintances complained to the paper that these details should not have been made public. I felt the stigma and shame of suicide and mental illness. I knew then that I would not tell anyone how or why I had lost my mother. I would avoid any topic near the subject for the next twenty years.

The next few years brought different feelings at different times. Sometimes some of the sadness changed to anger at my mother for not loving us enough to stay with us. I got angry at her for letting one of us find her. Sometimes I felt angry at my father for not seeing the seriousness of the situation and doing something to intervene. Then I would feel guilty for blaming him. I realized he didn't even deserve the guilt that he was probably already carrying.

Because my father became very isolated after the suicide, it felt like we were abandoned by both parents at the same time. From that point on, my sister Christa and I practically raised ourselves. I feel that we fortunately had enough love and nurturing during the important primary years to hold ourselves together during the years that followed.

When I was seventeen and she was twenty, Christa and I went to Germany to visit our relatives. We were visiting at Tante Ellie's house and my Tante Elsa walked in. Tante Elsa is my mother's twin sister. Christa became hysterical, crying and trying to catch her breath. She ran into the other room. I went in after her and asked her if she was okay. She was shaking and said she just wanted to be alone and just needed some time to calm down. I knew what was wrong. Having my mother's twin sister present was too much of a reminder for my sister.

At that moment, I wished that I had been the one who found my mother. As emotional and sensitive as I am, my sister is even more so. My dear sweet sister who would never hurt anyone had been subjected to so much horror. Suicide victims may regret that their death will hurt others, but their pain is so intense that the regret is put aside. I then had a better understanding of why we were avoiding the subject of my mother's death. It just brought too much pain; more pain than we ever wanted to inflict on each other.

In Germany, my grandmother talked to Christa and I alone about Mutti. She cried and said she didn't know my mother was so unhappy and having such trouble adjusting to a new and strange country. My father told her that neighbors had reported a taxi picking her up sometimes and suggested that maybe she had a terminal illness that she kept secret. Yes, she did. Her terminal illness was manic depression, better known today as bipolar disorder. Although it is not a terminal illness for everyone, it was for Mutti. Stigma and isolation stopped her from getting help, and trauma made it worse.

I realized at some point that I really lost my mother long before she had died by suicide. She withdrew herself from the rest of the family years before her death. She was suffering, and losing her was a gradual process. Gradually, I had been brought up less by her and more by my father and sisters. I never shared my theory of my mom having a mental illness so I don't even know if my Papa shared that belief. Unfortunately, mental illness is a subject that usually stays in the closet.

The following except is taken from the book *Coping with Suicide*:

> Suicide can be described as an interpersonal act. It is killing oneself, yet it also kills part of everyone who is close to or loves the person who dies. The emotional pain for the suicide victim is over, but is only the beginning for the survivors. The feelings themselves can be scary. Those feelings, as scary and awful as they are, have to be experienced and worked through for the grief to subside. Grief work is strenuous work. Time heals all wounds? In the case of grief, time helps, but time alone won't heal. It is a struggle that requires a lot of effort. Time spent mourning should not be limited to three months or six months or nine months. You need to give yourself permission to take a long time—as long as it takes.
>
> It may be disheartening to learn that it can take such a long time. One may wonder how in the world they are going to be able to stand it. The pain does not stay as sharp as it was in the beginning, and there may come a time when you don't think about it constantly for periods of time. On the other hand, it may bring a sense of relief to know it is okay to cry all over again when

something reminds you of your loss and the untimely death. The void will always be there with a memory, and for that reason mourning may never be complete. The comfort and hope come as life becomes different and the void no longer dominates your being. You will never be able to go back to life as it was before. If all goes well, you will be able to recover, but you will be different. You will learn from a grief experience. Unfortunately, learning to face and survive a loss is a painful lesson.

It is difficult to understand why anyone would choose to die. Mental instability comes with intense emotions. A person may be in crisis regardless of the importance of the situation to anyone else. The emotions typically experienced in a crisis are intense anger, fright, or sadness. These emotions block a person's ability to use cognitive or reasoning abilities. It becomes extremely difficult to make decisions or concentrate. It is not unusual for a person in crisis to declare how confused everything seems to be. Behavior may seem irrational as the person in crisis acts without the ability to foresee the consequences because of impaired judgment. Thinking becomes constricted. Instead of seeing possibilities, the mind decides there is no middle ground. Someone in crisis may focus on suicide as the only alternative. It is the light at the end of the tunnel, because cessation of consciousness signifies the end of suffering.

Perhaps the most significant characteristic of someone in crisis is despair and hopelessness. The hopelessness says that it will never get better and the thought of enduring the suffering forever is unbearable. Closely allied with hopelessness is helplessness. The person in crisis sees himself as having no control or power over what is happening. Furthermore, the sense of hopelessness complicates the whole situation. "Nothing will change, nothing will improve—so why try anymore?" Intense emotions affect the reasoning. When in crisis, people lose touch with the power to make choices and solve problems. Another important aspect of crisis theory is isolation. "No one cares, no one understands." It is so much more difficult to shoulder burdens alone.

Clinical depression and bipolar are common causes of suicide. Situational depression is a normal expression of disappointment and disappears with the passage of time and other distractions. It is normal to react to disappointment and failure with sadness and inner anger. However, clinical depression is a deep, despairing experience. It sometimes leaves a person struggling with a decision between living and dying. A feeling of worthlessness and low self-esteem accompanies deep depressive states. It can be due to a chemical imbalance in the body that affects the brain. It can be treated with medicines and psychotherapy.

Both schizophrenia and bipolar I disorder can be accompanied by psychosis and hallucinations. This may trigger a suicide attempt. The person may not be able to distinguish between what is real and what is not real. He or she gradually withdraws into himself, paying attention to his inner self, which may include voices that no one else hears. His or her outward behavior makes no sense to anyone else. They may become violent and harm themselves or others. (Judie Smith 1986)

The Fire

TWO MONTHS AFTER MY MOTHER DIED, we were awakened in the middle of the night by banging on our bedroom door. We opened to see flames reaching from the floor to the ceiling with Papa behind the flames shouting at us to climb out the window. Christa couldn't get the window open because paint was making it stick so she took her hands and broke the glass. All three of us: me, Christa, and Ruth, climbed out through the jagged glass. My papa tried to fight the fire with the hose until the firemen came and started to yell at him to get out of the house.

Much of the house was destroyed and we had to move to a rental for a few months.

What amazes me is my Papa's resilience during all these catastrophes. He never fell apart. He knew we needed him to take care of us. He was, after all, accustomed to a life of tragedy, beginning when he was a boy and lost his three-year-old brother to typhoid. He had lost a lot of pride in his mother country during the war. He lost the companionship of his mother and siblings when he decided to bring his family to America. He gave away the house he had built for our family to his sister. The only payment she had to make was a promise to always take care of their mother. After six years in America, he lost his wife to suicide. A few years later, he lost his mother, without the opportunity to be there for her.

My Papa had lots of stories to tell us when he was feeling strong enough. He was drafted to the German Army during World War II. His job during the war was to patrol the German/Russian border on cross-country skis. World War II started in 1939 when German forces invaded Poland under Hitler's rule. Papa once told me he would rather hide from the enemy than confront them and have to shoot someone. He also told me the story of a German woman named Ingeborg that lived on the German/Russian border. She would hide the German soldiers in her home so they wouldn't be shot by the Russian soldiers. She was subjected to rape by the Russian soldiers to save the German soldiers' lives. My middle name is Ingeborg. My papa said he named me after her because she was so brave and saved his life. In every war there are oppressors and suffering on both sides.

When the war was coming to an end, Papa's family lived in the territory of the Russian occupation. Their family's home was taken by the Russians, who shot the family dog during the process. That home still exists, but is now in Polish territory instead of German. Papa's father and brother never returned from a Russian prisoner-of-war camp. Papa escaped on his way to a Russian camp by jumping off a train. It is documented that in territories that were occupied by American soldiers, civilians and prisoners of war were treated much more humanely. Russia was an ally of the United States, but also had their own interests of spreading communism throughout Europe.

As I got a little bit older and learned more about history, I began to put all these stories together and realized that Papa fought for the Nazi army. I was afraid to ask him about this detail that he always left out of his stories, but I had to know, so one day I did.

"Papa, were you a Nazi?"

I never saw Papa get angry, but he was. "I had to be or I would die!"

"Do you still have your uniform?" I asked.

"I burned it!"

He was quiet the rest of the night. He was upset and I'm sure he had sensed the surprise and disappointment in my voice. But I wasn't disappointed in him. All the stories started to come together, and I understood more than ever why we had come to America. I'm sure Papa feared that somewhere in Russia and East Germany his name was on a list of escaped prisoners of war. There was never a doubt in my mind that Papa would not hurt anyone intentionally. He was the most gentle man I knew. It made sense that he had hid in the wilderness from the enemy on cross-country skis. To Papa, they were not the enemy. They were all young soldiers forced to fight for something they may not have even believed in. What many people don't realize is that there were countless everyday Germans that resisted Hitler's rule. With even the smallest act of defiance against the Nazis was the risk of torture and death, but many still took the risk. It wasn't until I was older that I realized where Papa's strength to deal with future trauma originated.

After a few months, the repairs were made on our home and we were able to move back in. By that time, Ruth's behavior began to become a little strange. She was buying sexy bikinis and lingerie from Fredericks of Hollywood and would strut around the house in them during the day. One of the symptoms of untreated bipolar disorder that no one likes to speak of is hypersexuality during the manic phase. This was before the times of online dating, but instead there were personal dating ads in the papers. Soon Ruth was packed and on a plane to California to move in with a handsome high school science teacher who was only too happy to welcome her after he saw her photographs. Boy, I bet he regretted that.

It wasn't long after she moved in with him that he was demanding she leave. Ruth informed us that he had told her to stop calling him and coming to see him at work, and that he got fired because of her interruptions during the work day. Poor guy. He didn't see that coming. He probably had to change his address, phone number, and everything else before she finally left him alone.

Ruth stayed in the California area. Over the next couple of years she dated several men until she met Richard and got pregnant in 1968. She and Rich planned to get married. She had asked my Uncle Kurt and Aunt Ina, who were living in California as well, to be the witnesses. She sent us a photograph of the four of them out to dinner when she introduced Richard to the only family she had in California. They all looked very happy. We were thrilled about the baby. But the marriage never happened. Elissa Ruth was born on July 17, 1969. Ruth and Richard had already broken up, and Richard denied paternity.

So, Ruth returned home to our house in Oakland as a single mom. Christa and I were so excited to have a baby in the house, but Papa, not so much. We had a small two-bedroom house, not at all suitable for all of us. Papa gave up his bedroom to Ruth and Elissa for a while and slept on the sofa, but it wasn't long before Papa and Ruth were on edge with each other. Christa and I loved having baby Elissa around; we didn't care how crowded it was!

Within a couple of months, Ruth found a lovely apartment in Oak Ridge, New Jersey. It was in half of a house, the rent was more than reasonable, it was furnished beautifully, and it was walking distance to the grocery store and a New York City bus stop. It was perfect. Ruth didn't have her driver's license, so she always used bus transportation to New York to go to work. She told us that Richard had helped her learn to drive and get her driver's permit in California, but she got into a terrible accident. I don't know if she got her driving privilege revoked or she was just too afraid to drive after that. She never gave us many details about the accident.

Ruth soon found a job in New York and a babysitter for Elissa. Christa and I visited her often. Christa and I adored Elissa. She was a cherub of a baby with ash-blonde curls. Ruth stayed in Oak Ridge for about three years before she got impatient again. Richard had relocated to Oklahoma, and Ruth decided she was going to go there and file a lawsuit for paternity and child support. So off she went.

Richard was a lawyer. Ruth took him to court for paternity and child support but lost. Richard proved that Ruth was dating other men close to the time of her pregnancy. She appealed, but lost again. The DNA tests proved that it was 99 percent positive that Richard was the father, but not 100 percent. This, I assume, started a deep decline in Ruth's mental health.

But life went on. I suppose some of Papa's stamina had rubbed off on us. The structure of our family consistently changed, but Papa was there doing what he needed to do for his daughters despite his frequent physical and emotional absence. Papa worked six days a week and through his one-week vacation so he would get paid double. The only vacations I went on were with my friends' families.

It turns out, Papa was right about Oakland: it really was a great place to grow up. We had fresh air and roads with little traffic and lots of kids our age. We went out and played in the street every night we could: Spud, soccer, Kick the Can, Red

Light-Green Light, Mother May I. It was very safe and none of our parents worried about us being out alone. And on the rare occurrence of a car coming by, it was "Car, car, c-a-r, stick your head in a jelly jar"! Such innocence.

As we got a little older, we ventured away from the neighborhood, but we still walked everywhere. The Ramapo River flowed through Oakland, adding beauty and an appreciation of nature for kids of the town. A popular activity was renting a canoe down at Cal's on the river for fifty cents an hour. We also had Pleasureland and Muellers Park right next to each other. They were big pools with pavilions and a building that provided great activities for the kids. We bought swimming memberships to one of the pools and we met friends there. In the evenings, there were dances at the Pleasureland Pool Pavillion, outdoor movies at Muellers Park, and in one of their barns, there was The Fish, a nightclub with no alcohol on weekends during the summer. The bands that played at Pleasureland were great! Some of them we even got to see before they became famous, one being Earth, Wind & Fire. On Friday nights we either went to a dance or roller-skating. Leaning on the support of our friends we became resilient teenagers despite our struggles and losses.

Bob

BOB AND I FIRST MET in seventh grade. We were always in the same homeroom because it was alphabetical (Jaehnel and LeDuc). I eyed him across my homeroom classroom in his Boy Scout uniform, but he was very quiet so I really didn't get to know him until the following year. In eighth grade he grew taller and more handsome. He ditched the Boy Scout uniform and gained a new confidence and new look with tighter pants, boots, and a hair swoop. He was quite the lady's man. He had flirted with me, but I didn't think he was my type.

One night, all of our friends went ice-skating on the big lake and had a big bonfire. Bob was a great skater, and suddenly my heart melted for him each time he wrapped his arms around me to skate with him. We ended up kissing on one of the docks and I was in love. We went to the eighth-grade prom together. His Mom drove us to Jahn's with our closest friends. Jahn's was an iconic ice cream place and we shared a "kitchen sink," which was a popular group dessert.

I think Bob and I truly were in love, but we fell in love too young. We spent the next four years dating each other and other people. Every person I dated I compared to Bob. After a period of dating others, we always missed each other and had dramatic reconciliations. I remember once we saw each other at a Pleasureland dance and ran into each other's arms—like we both knew it was time we made up and got together again. Just like in the movies.

And so, it would begin again. We would go back together and break up and continue on that cycle until I was seventeen and he was eighteen. That summer I was dating a guy named Clay. He was handsome and sweet. His parents were moving to California and he was going with them. Our last date before he left, we went to Hens Roost, which was one of the places we all hung out. Bob was there with some friends and saw Clay and me there, getting something to eat.

Clay's family was staying at a hotel before they moved, so Clay and I went to his room after. We talked, and Clay wanted me to move to California after I graduated high school and eventually marry him. I didn't know what to say. He was so much more serious than I was. I told him it was too premature and we were too young to be thinking of that. The night after Clay left, Bob called me on the phone. He told me that he couldn't stop thinking about me since he saw me and Clay together at the Hens Roost. "I realized how much I loved you and I hated seeing you with someone else." It was one of those times we both knew we needed to be with each other again.

This time we never broke up.

One night, on our way home from a double date with another couple, Bob and I were passengers in our friend's car when the driver got into a terrible accident. I was taken by ambulance to the hospital. There was an EMT who was especially nice to me. He wrapped me in blankets and held my hand.

He wouldn't let Bob come in the ambulance. He stayed with me the entire time at the hospital even during my x-rays. Needless to say, Bob didn't like him. When my father got to the hospital, the EMT introduced himself to Papa and told him what happened. My Papa loved him! Papa hated Bob's longish hair and this guy was clean-cut. Papa actually took his phone number and the next day said I should call him and thank him. "That's his job, Papa." "Nooo," Papa said, "he went above and beyond for you." I never called him, much to Papa's dismay. I spent the next couple of weeks healing at home with a sprained ankle, a lot of torn ligaments, and stitches in a few places in my face where glass needed to be removed.

Near the end of high school, when all of my friends were contemplating their future colleges and careers, all I could think of was the family and home that I wanted. I dreamed of a cute, cozy home in the country with two little children, a boy and a girl. I was already dating Bob, the person I wanted to marry. We had a blast dating. We were always doing a lot of different things: going to carnivals, fishing, canoeing, snowmobiling, skiing, concerts, Steak 'n Brew every Friday night and Burger King and Baskin Robbins every Sunday night. Bob's dad had a forty-two-foot cabin cruiser that he kept down the shore so we used to go out in it every weekend during the summer. Sometimes we went out for an overnight ride and slept on the top level under the stars. We made pyramids on the beach with Bob's brothers and their girlfriends and spent time at the marina pool. We loved going to Max's for the footlong hotdogs, Longo's for the subs, and The Clam Hut for daily double lobsters. We were in love and had any number of adventures at our fingertips.

We were engaged six months after we graduated high school and married one year after that. I was working as a secretary at Ramapo College and attending classes in the evening. Bob had been working in his dad's home gutter manufacturing and installation business since he started working as a teenager in the summers, but hoped to either get into the art field or start a business of his own. Bob was an extremely talented cartoon artist and was constantly doodling caricatures.

The void created by the lack of a normal family life growing up was a burning desire I needed to fill. Our marriage was June 24, 1972. It was a happy occasion for us even though we did not have the blessings of Papa and my future mother-in-law. My in-laws were going through a terrible divorce and my mother-in-law could just not handle her oldest son leaving the home as well. Papa thought we were too young and not yet financially secure enough. Maybe we didn't make enough to save but we made enough to live and that's all we cared about. He also didn't like Bob much, as I mentioned, because of his longish hair. He insisted that if Bob didn't get a haircut for the wedding he would not come and give me away. Looking back at the pictures I can kind of see my Papa's point of view. Especially since Bob's hair seemed to grow outward instead of down.

We had a beautiful outdoor wedding at Carmel Retreat in Mahwah. My sister Christa was my maid of honor, and my two best friends, Debbie and Linda, were also bridesmaids. Linda later ended up as my sister-in-law. Christa was finishing college and would be married the following year. All of Bob's brothers and my future brother-in-law were also in my wedding. So even though we were missing my mother and Ruth, we were surrounded by family. My father relented and came and gave me away at the wedding. Our reception was originally planned at Bob's mom's house, but it got too complicated to pull it off. Bob's mom wouldn't allow Bob's dad to come with his new wife, and Bob's dad wouldn't come without her. We ended up just having a small after-party with family—including my father, the wedding party, and some close friends—at Bob's mom's house. Bob's dad and wife were not there, but Bob and I went to dinner with them later that evening. Despite all the family issues our marriage caused, we were as happy as could be and couldn't wait to begin our married life together. I promised myself that when I had children and it was time for them to marry, they would have whatever they wanted for their wedding. I wouldn't interfere but only support them.

For our honeymoon, we rented a house on a lake in Ludlow, Vermont. I found it in the Vermont Chamber of Commerce booklet that I had sent away for. These were different times, after all. There was no searching on the Internet for vacation homes. We pulled up to a quaint farm, towing our little motorboat behind. The owner said we had a few choices: we could have a room in their farmhouse, or our choice of three cabins right on the lake . . . but he warned us that they were rustic. We said, "Oh, we're on our honeymoon. We prefer our own cabin!" So, we drove down to the lake to look at the cabins.

The first cabin was rustic, to say the least. There was no kitchen! The beds were single bunks, with only two of them having thin mattresses. We said, "Oh, this won't do! We need a kitchen." The last cabin had a kitchen, but the sleeping arrangements were just as rustic. We said, "Oh, this won't do, we're on our honeymoon! We want a bed we can both sleep in together." We asked for a refund. The farmer said there was one more option: his parents' farmhouse on the lake. They had both passed away but they hadn't done anything with the house yet. We looked at the farmhouse. It was right on the lake and there were no other habited homes on the lake. It had three bedrooms upstairs and was quaintly furnished, with a beautiful fireplace. We said, "We'll take it!" I felt like Goldilocks!

Once we settled in, we realized that they really had not done *anything* to the house since the owners had passed. All their belongings were still in the drawers and closets.

Bob and I picked the bedroom that we thought would be the most comfortable. The first night we couldn't sleep. We both felt like we were being watched. I said, "I feel like somebody doesn't want us in this bed." Bob said he felt the same way. The next two nights we tried the other two bedrooms with the same results. We finally took our sleeping bags and spread them out in front of the fireplace, and that's where we spent the other nights.

We took some of our wedding money and bought two cross-country bikes. We pedaled them for miles across the countryside and brought home wild flowers for the vases in the house. It was a fairytale honeymoon. I felt like I could have lived there forever.

One night, we went out for dinner. When we came home, the outside light was on for us. We knew we hadn't turned them on, and these were the days before sensor lights. The next time we saw the farmer we asked him if he had put the lights on for us. He said no, that he hadn't been to the house. Another night, when we decided to get some groceries and have dinner in, I turned on the burner for the stove and a different burner came on for a few seconds.

Bob and I decided that the spirits of this couple were still in this house. But we were not afraid. As long as we respected their belongings, they did not mind us staying in their home. We began to try to get to know them by looking at some of their belongings. They seemed like a couple very much in love with each other, with an appreciation for nature's beauty and the simple things in life. At one point I was looking through some of her recipes. I thought, what a shame that she lovingly wrote these recipe cards by hand and no one would be sharing them or passing them down. So, I took some with me and still have them in my recipe box. Somehow, I had the feeling that this woman of the house was happy that I was taking them. This was our start. Our children and the rest of our lives were still only our hopes and dreams.

A New Addition to the Family

THE YEAR AFTER I GOT MARRIED, my sister Christa got married to her high school sweetheart as well. My father joined Parents without Partners and met a lovely woman, Marilyn. They were married the next year. She had two sons who became our stepbrothers, Walt and Bill. We were so happy for Papa. No one deserved some happiness more than him.

For a while my life proceeded as planned. However, our first child did not end up being the little newborn baby we dreamed of, but Ruth's daughter, Elissa, who was now six years old. While Bob and I were on vacation in Maine, my sister Christa received a call from a family friend in Oklahoma where Ruth and Elissa were living. He explained that Ruth had locked herself in her room and was not caring for Elissa and suggested that someone from the family come to get Elissa before she ended up in foster care. Since I was away camping in Maine and this was before cell phones, by default, my sister Christa was on a plane to Oklahoma to try to rescue our niece, Elissa. This was not a simple task, as Ruth did not give up her daughter easily, even though she was not in her right mind. Christa ended up having to get a lawyer and spend several days having Ruth involuntary committed. As luck would have it, it happened to be the lawyer that lost the paternity suit for Ruth against Elissa's father. He had a lot of sympathy for what had happened and didn't charge Christa for his services. He said he very much believed that Richard was Elissa's father. She looked very much like him. He recommended that Christa whisk Elissa away to New Jersey without contacting the state foster care system. Although the State does explore relatives as potential foster parents, it is a long and tedious process, especially interstate placements.

After this terrible ordeal that my sister Christa had to navigate in Oklahoma, I thought the least I could do was offer to have Elissa to stay with us. I was between jobs at the time and after all, it would be temporary, right? I was twenty-two years old and did not yet have my psychology and teaching education. I, along with most other people in the world, had very little knowledge or understanding of mental illness.

I still had hope and compassion for my sister Ruth. I still believed her condition would improve. I called her at the hospital in Oklahoma and wrote her letters letting her know how Elissa was doing and encouraging her to try to get well. I couldn't imagine anything worse than losing your child. Elissa was, amazingly, a very happy child. I don't think I realized until I had my own children how unusual it is for a child to be so happy after a separation with their parent. I did see it occur many times during my work as a social worker when some of the children were removed from their families. It appears sometimes that maternal attachment is not fully developed.

The hospital diagnosed Ruth with schizophrenia. After about six months, I talked to hospital staff who said Ruth was ready for discharge but she would need to be released to someone that would be responsible for her. I reluctantly agreed. How could I say no? I had her daughter.

They arranged for her flight, and all five of us picked her up at the airport: Bob and I, Elissa, Christa, and Christa's husband, Bo. Ruth stayed with us for a while until we found her a room to rent temporarily. Bob and I lived in a very small apartment, and Ruth's condition was not nearly as improved as we expected. Moreover, it seemed to be getting worse. So, she lived in a rented room in a big house down the road from us. I would take her to all her appointments—Social Security, welfare, unemployment insurance, and apartment searching—and then rush back each day to meet Elissa's school bus at 3:00.

We finally came across an apartment in Ruth's price range about half an hour away in Boonton. She was excited to have Elissa live with her again, but we suggested she first try to settle in the apartment on her own. Ruth grew more and more impatient and we couldn't prolong it any longer; Elissa wanted to go. After all, she still loved her mother. We visited, but with each visit we became more and more concerned about Ruth's instability.

At a loss for what to do, our situation was resolved by Ruth herself. One day she dropped by with a man in a truck and said she was leaving Elissa with us. I assumed it was someone she met in the dating want-ads. She was moving to Connecticut with this man but he would not bring any kids with them. I lost a lot of compassion for Ruth. Here I was trying to help her keep her daughter and she was actually giving her away. I wondered what this man wanted. Five or so years back Ruth was beautiful and charming but her mental illness had definitely changed her. She had stopped taking care of herself and had a disconnected look and demeanor. All I could think was, "Thank God he didn't want Elissa."

One day, a few months later, the gentleman from Connecticut dropped off Ruth and all her stuff in our driveway and tore out of there like a bat out of hell. I had never seen her this bad. She rocked back and forth in a chair and couldn't talk. She was unable to tell us about anything that had transpired the last couple of months. We had no other option but to bring Ruth to the state psychiatric hospital, Greystone.

It was such a sad place. Many of the patients we saw were rocking and staring into space. I felt so sad for Ruth and the other patients. We visited Ruth a few more times, even though I dreaded it each time. Sometimes she was just coming out of shock treatments when we visited. What a cruel existence. Those blank faces haunted me day and night. After several months there, she was placed in an apartment in Orange, New Jersey. I believe someone was assigned to check in on her. They didn't ask me to take her home this time. Her disease had progressed to the point that it was too much for me to handle.

One day I called the Orange apartment to see how she was doing and her landlord told me she was gone. We had no idea where she'd gone until we got a phone call from a hospital in California. Ruth had been found sleeping under a bridge and was brought to the hospital by the police. I started crying as I told the person at the other end of the phone, "I can't take her and I don't know what to do. We've tried so many times." To my surprise, she calmed me down and told me it was okay. "We are calling to better understand her situation. We need history and information. We understand that you can't take her. It's okay." I told them all I knew. Bob and I had just bought our first house and had recently moved into our cozy home in the country. It was then we began to realize Elissa would be a permanent part of our family.

Family

In April 1977, I felt a soreness in my breasts. We had been trying for a few months to get pregnant. I went to the doctor and waited for the results of my pregnancy test. When they called and told me it was positive, I jumped up and down with joy. We were so happy. I soon started to feel flutters in my belly and already felt a connection to this little person who was made in love and was a combination of Bob and me. Being pregnant brought me so much joy. I had a flush in my cheeks. My hair and nails were so healthy. I felt this beautiful life inside me and it showed on the outside. I never complained about being pregnant. To me, it was a miracle.

On November 14, 1977, my son was born. He was nineteen inches and six pounds, thirteen ounces. Jeremy was such a beautiful baby. The nurses in the hospital whispered to me secretly that he was the cutest baby in the nursery. The first month was so easy, too. He wanted to nurse every four hours and in between he slept so peacefully.

Bob and I were so happy. Becoming a mother was the most magical time of my life.

Then Jeremy woke up to the world and he was no longer happy. He seemed to cry constantly, like he was in pain. I thought maybe he wasn't getting enough milk so I gradually stopped nursing and switched to formula, but it didn't help. I thought he must have colic or a milk allergy. He cried when I stopped to burp him. He just wanted to drink his bottle down and often had projectile vomiting. I explained this to his pediatrician but he passed it off as my being a new, first-time mom, and said, "Feed him as much as he wants—he'll let you know when he's full. Some babies just cry more than others."

So, I did, and there were plenty of days when I cried along with him. When he started on baby cereal, he cried in between bites. My little baby got so chubby. When I went back to the pediatrician for Jeremy's next check-up, he more or less told me he was overweight and I needed to feed him less. Under my breath, I cursed that doctor and wished he would make up his mind.

When Jeremy was five months old, I felt some movement in my belly and soreness in my breasts and I knew I was pregnant again. I cried when I told Bob. This mother thing was so difficult, how could I handle two babies? But soon Jeremy began to smile more often and his pain seemed to abate. We started to look forward to our second child, who was born when Jeremy was thirteen months old. Jaehnel was born on December 15, 1978, six weeks early, weighing in at only five pounds, three ounces. Her weight went down a few ounces, which is typical in the first few days. She was down to four pounds, 11 ounces, and I couldn't take her home until her weight stabilized. She had jaundice, so she had to be under the lights in the nursery all the time. This meant she had to have this huge, bulky bandage over her eyes for the lights. They couldn't keep taking the bandages off and on her eyes because her skin would get irritated, so they stayed on all the time. She looked so uncomfortable and cried all the time. I cried too, and begged them to take the bandages off. I wanted to look into those baby blue eyes, but I couldn't.

Bob came to visit me every night and left Jeremy with Elissa and my neighbor.

Inevitably, my baby girl had to stay in the hospital a week longer than I did. It was a horrible feeling leaving the hospital in a wheelchair without my baby. I felt like people looked at me as if my baby had died.

Elissa was eight years old when Jeremy was born and initially very excited to have a little brother. When Jaehnel came along, the novelty wore off. Having two babies thirteen months apart took an awful lot of our attention. Elissa, being the only child in our family at the time, was used to a lot of attention. An eight- or nine-year-old still needs a lot of attention, and we tried to give all three of our children all the attention they needed, but sometimes it felt like we just didn't have enough to go around. I think Elissa often felt like she didn't belong and wanted to be part of someone else's family. The three children always loved each other, though.

Jeremy loved Jaehnel from the moment we brought her home. Jeremy made up for the misery he experienced as an infant when he became the happiest toddler I had ever seen. He became Jaehnel's protector and best friend. It was so much fun to watch him and his sister together. We encouraged adventure, like our parents did. They were always building forts with blankets and pillows and setting up booby traps in their room. They had such an enthusiasm for life. They also loved to dress up. Jeremy loved to wear his favorite striped bathrobe open without the belt. This way when he jumped off the sofa it would fly in the air like a cape. He would wear it with a cowboy hat and an eye mask and would declare to be "The Mad Stranger." I now look back at what an ironic nickname this was. It's like he already knew something about himself that we didn't know yet.

The joy we had as a family was beautiful, but also a strain on our relationship with Elissa. We wanted her to be happy in our family but I understand how hard it was for her too, with the age difference between her and the two babies. We were also much younger than her friends' parents. I was only sixteen years older than Elissa, and I always looked much younger than my age. I was twenty-three years old and I looked sixteen. When I went to Elissa's first parent-teacher conference, the teacher said to me, "How old are you?" Sometimes people made me feel like I had a lot of nerve acting like a parent to Elissa. I guess it's no mystery why Elissa seemed to feel that way, too.

The activities for two- and three-year-olds are quite different than that of a ten-year-old, and it was often difficult to make it work. We made her go camping with us, to Disney World and on other vacations, usually against her will. We loved her tremendously and eventually realized we couldn't say, "You're going to come with us and be happy and have fun." We gradually stopped forcing her and we became quite distanced in her teenage years, but as I said, we all did the best we could. Nothing could spoil the love, gratitude and joy we had for our children.

I have such a sweet memory of my Jeremy and Jaehnel in preschool. I wasn't working out of the home yet, but I sent to preschool one or two mornings a week for socialization and so I could have some one-on-one time with each of them. The first day I started Jaehnel in preschool she was two-and-a-half years old. She was so attached to me and so shy, so I thought this would be good for her. She cried when Jeremy and I brought her into the classroom and wouldn't let us leave. She finally took Jeremy's hand and the teacher said Jeremy could stay if it made her feel comfortable. I left but stayed in the building just in case. When I came back and looked through the window, there they were, Jaehnel holding onto

Jeremy's hand while they participated in all the activities. Her big brother, all of three-and-a-half years old. He was her protector way back then and continued to be through the years, even giving some of her boyfriends a hard time.

An Accurate Diagnosis

At some point after Ruth was released from the hospital, we received a call from the West Milford Police. Ruth had flown from California to New Jersey and taken a taxi to West Milford where my sister Christa lived. I believe she didn't know my sister's address so the taxi driver ended up driving her to the police station. She expected my sister to pick her up but Christa and her husband refused, so the police called us. I felt so sorry for her; it was hard to say no. I hoped her state of mind was somewhat stable, but my hopes were in vain and she wasn't doing well at all. At this point, Jaehnel was two, Jeremy was three, and Elissa was eleven.

Bob brought her to our home but it only took a few minutes to realize the extent of her instability and that night Bob took Ruth to the Newton Hospital where she was evaluated and hospitalized in the psychiatric unit. Perhaps my sister and husband made the right decision. I believe that my sister, Christa, realized before I did, because of her experience in Oklahoma, how useless our attempts to save Ruth were. Her psychiatrist, Dr Feldman, called the next day for information about Ruth's psychiatric history. I told him that she was diagnosed with schizophrenia. I visited her and brought her clothes. Dr. Feldman asked us questions about our family mental health history. He said he thought Ruth had bipolar instead of schizophrenia. This was about 1981 and research was starting to reveal that bipolar I disorder (the most severe form) could be accompanied with hallucinations. Prior to this, patients with hallucinations were usually diagnosed with schizophrenia. When I told the doctor about my mother's suicide, he felt that his diagnosis was accurate. He wanted to start her on lithium, which was a fairly new medication for bipolar at the time. Ruth was refusing to take it so they wanted to administer it by injection.

Dr. Feldman repeatedly reminded me that Newton's psychiatric ward was short-term, with a two-week maximum stay. After two weeks, he said Ruth was not ready for discharge and they would need to transfer her to Greystone. He said there was one other possibility, but it was a long shot. The Homestead, which was more or less a nursing home for the elderly and disabled, had a vacant bed.

I picked Ruth up and took her for an interview. They accepted her and a few days later I was picking her up from the hospital and moving her in. The day I picked her up she was given a prescription bottle of lithium with instructions to follow up for refills. On our way out I said something about the importance of taking the medicine. Ruth said, "Oh that's for depression and I'm not depressed anymore. I don't need it." I knew we were doomed. We received a call that we needed to come get her a few days later. She was having a severe psychotic episode and was locked in her room banging on the walls. Poor Bob had to go and talk her into opening the door and he had to bring her to the hospital while I stayed home with the kids. Bob got more than he bargained for when he said for *better or worse*. The hospital wouldn't take her since she had just finished a two-week stay so they transferred her to Greystone for long-term care. Bob got home at two in the morning. It was the night before Jaehnel's third birthday party.

Somehow, Ruth ended up in California again and we didn't hear from her for a couple of years. Then one day, out of the blue, we received a call from the police in California. They had received a call from Ruth's landlord. No one had seen Ruth coming out of her apartment for months. They broke into her apartment and found her sitting on the toilet in a catatonic state. She must have been in that position for weeks. She was emaciated down to eighty-five pounds. She was rushed to the hospital where she was fed intravenously and spent months recovering. I cried and sobbed. I was so angry at this disease that had taken so much from my family.

The State of California realized that Ruth did not accept or recognize that she had bipolar, so given the choice, she would never willingly take the medicine prescribed to her. Individuals with Anosognosia (denial of mental illness) have a much lower chance of recovery or remission. The woman I spoke to at the hospital advised me not to take any responsibility for Ruth. She explained that as long as there was a family member willing to accept responsibility for her, they would be willing to relinquish her and that was not in anyone's best interest. She told me there was no way I should feel guilty about this because it really was the best thing for Ruth to remain safe. No one had ever explained it to me that way and I wanted to hug her through the phone. We had to sign papers that we were not willing to be her guardian. I felt like this sounded so mean, but it really was the best plan for her. They court ordered her into group home placement and court-ordered her to take her medicine as prescribed. I breathed a sigh of relief. The State of California was now Ruth's guardian. I don't think this would have ever happened in New Jersey.

I spoke quite often with the lady that ran the group home. She was very kind. She asked if Elissa could visit her mother because Ruth was doing a bit better and was consistently asking to see Elissa. It was summer and the woman's granddaughter was going to be visiting and was the same age as Elissa. She assured me that she would pick up Elissa at the airport and make sure she was safe at all times. Elissa wanted to go, so I agreed. I think somehow Elissa always expected to see her mom as she was before her illness.

So off she went to California. I believe she was twelve at the time. A few days later she called and said she wanted to come home early. She was upset. I talked to the group home supervisor who said she wasn't sure why. They had gone to Catalina Island and Disney World. She thought Elissa had had a good time but she appeared to be a little homesick. I talked to Ruth, who sounded agitated. She said Elissa just wanted to spend time with the granddaughter and she was supposed to be visiting her. Elissa ended up staying the full week but never asked to see her Mom again.

As soon as Dr. Feldman diagnosed Ruth with bipolar 1, I felt that my mother had been diagnosed as well. I became hungry for knowledge about this disease, and learned it was 85% caused by genetics. It had plagued my mother and sister and would haunt future generations of my family. I learned that bipolar is also known as manic depression, which refers to the high and low poles of the illness. These occur when the brain chemical dopamine soars to higher than normal levels and also dips down to lower than normal levels. The periods of highs and lows vary from person to person but can last days, weeks, or months. The disease also varies greatly in other ways. Bipolar II is less severe than bipolar I but still a very serious and disruptive disease. Some people also suffer from rapid cycles or mixed states.

To people who haven't experienced this, an elevated mood might sound like fun but it can quickly pass from being euphoric or irritable to abnormal, irrational behavior accompanied by hallucinations and delusions. Other symptoms include rapid, loud, pressured speech, flighty ideas, disconnect with reality, overspending, hypersexuality, grandiose self-image, and substance use.

Most people with this disease can experience periods of stability without medication between the episodes of mania and depression. Medication can help provide continued stability, helping to avoid episodes or making episodes less severe. The right combination of medication can be tricky, especially because the disease is so labile and medication adjustments usually need to be made. Antidepressants for the depressive episodes need to be taken with caution because they can cause manic episodes. More recently, antidepressants specifically for bipolar have become available that do not trigger mania.

There are approximately six million people in the US that suffer from bipolar disorder. That is about 2.5 percent of the population, and only includes diagnosed cases. The disease usually surfaces between late teens and twenties, but it's possible to have early or late onset.

Depressive episodes of the disease look very much like symptoms of clinical depression or major depressive disorder. This includes feelings of despair, worthlessness, lack of energy, or inability to enjoy the things enjoyed in the past (Web MD "Bipolar Disorder/Mental Health")

Many people believe that the risk of suicide is most common in this state of despair, but I tend to believe that the risk is present in both manic and depressive episodes. I imagine mania being a very traumatic, scary experience, like a nightmare that you want to put to an end.

A New Home

In 1985, Bob and I bought our second home in Hardwick. We loved it even though it needed a complete remodel. I pictured it with new natural cedar siding and a white rail around the house with an added garage and decking. We tackled it with every ounce of love and eventually we did turn it into a beautiful modern farmhouse-style home.

Jaehnel was in kindergarten full time. It was the first time all the kids were in school all day and I decided it was a good time for me to go back to school. As I selected my classes, there was a course I wanted to take but was also afraid. It fit into my schedule so well that I signed up for it. It was called Death and Dying. It involved writing a ten-page term paper at the end of the course about our greatest loss. Of course, I wrote about the loss of my mother. This was probably the first time I talked to anyone about my mother and how she had died. Somehow, talking to people that were somewhat removed from my situation made it easier. My professor was a therapist. Her mother had suffered from postpartum depression and had also died by suicide but when she was an infant. She shared that she grew up wondering if her mother had not loved her enough to stay.

I realized that I grew up thinking the same thing. My professor's openness allowed me to feel all the feelings, to forgive my mother and forgive myself. It became clear to me that her life experience had led her to her career choice. Even though I wanted to, I didn't voice much about my mother's death in class. It took writing about it first for me to be able to talk about it. My term paper had so much therapeutic value for me. This is when I realized writing was healing for me.

Life is a constant experience of the loss of my mother. When I hear others complain about their mothers, I wish I had one to complain about. I wish she had been there for me in all the moments I needed a mom: to offer advice, help plan my wedding, help me with my babies. I hope in her afterlife she can see the people her children grew up to be and I hope she can see her beautiful grandchildren and great-grandchildren.

I no longer feel angry or guilty. Lifting the blame has helped me to grieve my mother in a more positive way. I still feel sadness for her. I know I still have a lot of unresolved grief and I don't think it will ever be truly resolved.

For years I could not even talk about my mother. It was too painful for me to think about. I find that it is not painful anymore. I can now find it comforting to look at old pictures of my mother. It's nice to see her smiling and holding me on her lap as a baby. I can tell she was happy and that she loved me. When I got to the point of being able to frame some pictures of her and hang them up on the wall, this provoked a lot of questions from my kids about how she died. Ruth's experience had helped me understand my mother's experience. It was hard to find the words to tell my kids. I think I finally told them when they were about twelve and thirteen years old.

Jeremy: The Beginning of His Madness

ELISSA WENT AWAY TO COLLEGE from 1987-1992 at Montclair University. She did her student teaching in social studies and history secondary education at Morris Knolls High School in Denville and met her soulmate, Bob, another history teacher there. She got married in 1993. They had two beautiful children, Paige and Bobby, who are both successful teachers now. Elissa moved from teaching to guidance counselor and Bob moved from teaching to vice principal. They have a beautiful home. Elissa is an overachiever and generous giver. I tell her that in spite of our difficulties we must have done something right.

Jaehnel was a compassionate, caring child as well. She had an amazing artistic ability that she must have inherited from her dad. She started drawing incredible pictures when she was about two or three. Drawing was one of Jeremy and Jaehnel's favorite activities as kids. Jeremy's drawings were more mechanical. He drew scaled, detailed motors and engines with all the intricate parts drawn with unbelievable accuracy. Jaehnel knew she wanted to be an art teacher from the time she was about six, and never wavered. An art teacher is what she came to be and now teaches kindergarten through eighth grade.

I always encouraged all three of my kids in sports. Elissa and Jaehnel both played softball and basketball. Jeremy played soccer and football, and did wrestling as well. His interest in each one only lasted one year. He seemed to have performance anxiety and didn't like contact sports. He would build detailed villages with Legos. We thought for sure he would end up being some kind of engineer. He found his niche in mechanics, ATVs, cars, and motorcycles. By the time he was eleven, he was buying dirt bikes that needed work, fixing them up, and selling them. By the time he was sixteen, he had saved enough to buy his first car, a white Mustang, the same as his dad's first car.

All of Jeremy's teachers loved him. He was classified as "perceptually impaired" by the Child Study Team but I'm still not sure that was an accurate classification. He had special education classes but he never experienced the stigma of being in special education. His teachers were so great and made learning fun. Jeremy truly thought he was "special" in the best way. I remember one of his teachers saying that he was the nicest kid he ever knew in all of his years of teaching. We were so proud of Jeremy. This was quite a compliment coming from a teacher with thirty-five years of experience.

We went camping on the Lake George Islands almost every summer, and my kids loved it. They were all so happy there. The summer that Jeremy was fourteen and entering high school, it was just the four of camping. Elissa had stopped coming. She was working and living on her own at the time. Jeremy became very sad that summer when we were at Lake George. He kept hugging me and saying he didn't know what was wrong, but he didn't feel like himself. He started to cry and said he didn't really know why. I believe he had so much anxiety about starting high school. I worried about his mental health, especially knowing our family history.

Jeremy's anxiety continued, and when he started high school he struggled. He tried so hard. He would read his assignments in his textbooks and cry afterward saying he didn't understand anything he read. Instead of using his locker, Jeremy carried all his books in his backpack all day. He was so nervous that he would be late for his classes if he stopped at his locker. I felt so bad for him. He tried to do everything right. He tried so hard. He worried so much and his anxiety seemed to increase with time.

In May 1994, I graduated college. I was forty years old. We decided to take a celebration vacation to Jamaica. Unbeknownst to me, my two children had decided that they would try pot for the first time. They were fifteen and sixteen years old. Jamaica had a reputation of having the best pot available and plenty of it. We stayed in a villa that was owned by a friend of ours. He had employed several of the locals to keep the place running. There was a cook, a maid, a gardener, a night watchman, and a supervisor. We were treated like royalty. It was a beautiful villa with private tennis courts and an in-ground pool. There was also a view of the ocean, although we had to drive to the beach.

One night I found out that my kids had asked the gardener for pot. The gardener had asked my husband if it was okay, and he had given his permission. I wish he had asked me because I would have said no. When I found out, I told my kids that I wanted them to promise to never consider doing it again. That was naïve of me, for sure. Bob said I was overreacting and it was no big deal. He reminded me that we had indulged in a toke or two in our younger years and we were fine.

Over the next several months, I had suspicions that Jeremy had continued smoking pot. He was hanging out with different friends, and his behavior began to change. I would worry about it, and Bob would regard it all as normal teen experiences.

Less than a year later, his behavior became manic. I thought I had lost the son I knew. All of a sudden, I was asking God, "Where is my son?" His body was here but the son I knew was not inside! His behavior was so strange. He shaved the sides of his head and left it long on top. He wore a woven sweatshirt (called a drug rug) every day with long underwear. He didn't attend school. He walked around town with his drug rug, long underwear, and a big stereo on his shoulder. We took his car keys away because he was not stable enough to drive. He walked miles every day. It was embarrassing, but my concern for his safety overtook any concern about embarrassment.

One night he took off on his dirt bike and drove illegally all over the roads. My husband, Bob, tried to catch up with him in the car but Jeremy just raced around faster and his dad couldn't even catch up with him. When his dad finally caught up with him and convinced him to come home, we brought him to the hospital emergency room. He was evaluated and drug tested. He had several drugs inside his system. I was shocked. He did these drugs with other friends his age. He was diagnosed with manic depression, also known as bipolar disorder. I cried and cried. I guess I always knew it was a possibility that one of my children might have this disease that ran in my family.

We met with the psychiatrist, and Jeremy was started on medication. She explained that drugs, even marijuana, were very aggravating to bipolar disorder. It was recommended that Jeremy be hospitalized, and it was explained to Jeremy that the process would be much easier if he would admit himself voluntarily. He refused. He was in full-blown mania, but thought he was fine. He was happy drinking and smoking marijuana as much as he wanted. The doctor recommended that we have him committed if he didn't agree voluntarily, and we began the paperwork. The doctor advised Jeremy that he was going to be hospitalized anyway, because his parents were committing him. He looked at us like he couldn't believe what he was hearing. "You're going to have me committed to the hospital?" The doctor convinced him that he might as well sign in voluntarily because that way he could have a say in when he was discharged, so he reluctantly agreed. We drove him to Carrier Clinic in Belle Meade, New Jersey and checked him in to a dual diagnosis ward in the hospital. At the time, I thought this was the worst day of my life. It was April 9, 1995. This night reminded me in many ways of the night my sister Ruth was first hospitalized when she was seventeen. I had a new understanding of what my parents were going through.

I had taken to writing in a journal when I was feeling sad or worried. Shortly after Jeremy was diagnosed, I wrote in my journal:

From our memories, my family will learn, grow, and prevent our loved ones in future generations from succumbing to the power of this illness called manic depression. Never again will one of our family be engulfed in the madness to the point they will take their own life. Never again should one of our family resist treatment and deny illness to the point they must spend half of their life institutionalized. I hope my loving son will be the catalyst for changing our family's fate. When and if this illness strikes again, we will be knowledgeable and prepared. Future generations will look to Jeremy as the first to combat this family's affliction. He will be our source of hope.

The day he was born I knew he was sent for a very special reason. That's why I know he will win this battle. He's the one that has the strength to show himself the way to hope and recovery.

This was my wish, but would it come true?

Surgery

My father was due to go into the hospital in a few days for bypass surgery. They had found at least four blockages. The day he was going in for the surgery, we had to go to a meeting in Belle Mead for Jeremy. I lied to my father that I couldn't come to the hospital because I had a cold and didn't want to get him sick. I couldn't tell him about Jeremy. His heart was already so fragile. I was crying on the phone when I told him I loved him, so I sounded like I had a cold.

For the next week or so I drove to Manalowkin Hospital and Carrier Clinic on alternating days, visiting my father one day and Jeremy the next. Each were an hour and a half away from our house in opposite directions. My father had come through the surgery okay. When I visited him after the surgery, he seemed dazed and foggy from the morphine, but the surgeon said everything went well.

One day when my stepmother visited my father, the nurse advised her that he had fallen out of bed trying to get up to go to the bathroom. That night my stepmother became concerned because my father's condition was deteriorating. He was confused and delirious. She insisted that a cardiologist come see him, but there were none available so a neurologist came to see him and seemed unconcerned. He said these were common side effects from the morphine.

By the next morning, my father was unconscious. They put in a pump to get his heart pumping faster. Finally, they opened him up again and saw that the blood was coagulated around his heart. Pumping the heart had probably made his condition worse. I asked the doctor if this could be from falling and he said possibly, but they couldn't know for sure. My father had had six arteries bypassed during his surgery and the doctor said this could happen after open heart surgery and referred to it as a stroke. My friend's husband worked as a doctor in the hospital and he went to see my father. He said the fall was not even recorded.

Carrier Clinic had advised us that Jeremy would be discharged on the twentieth of April. The day Jeremy was discharged, he didn't seem much better to me at all. We took him right to the hospital to see my father. Jeremy really didn't seem to understand what was going on. I sat by my father and talked to him. I hoped he could hear me. My father was on life support. We had a family meeting the next day with the neurologist. He advised us that they did brain scans that revealed my father was brain dead. If he lived, he would be a vegetable. We knew he wouldn't want that, so we agreed to take him off life support. The next day he passed away.

My grief was so complicated with the worry that my son would never be himself again. I felt numb. Two great losses at the same time. I couldn't eat and lost a lot of weight. It took about two months after we hospitalized Jeremy for him to look at me like he loved me again.

Learning

I TRIED TO MEET with the vice principal at Jeremy's high school and explain that Jeremy had a mental illness that ran in our family and I hoped the school would do everything they could do to help him. He looked at me and said, "You know what I wish? I wish that all the kids that don't want to be in school would just leave and all the kids that want to do drugs, I wish they would just leave!" He definitely did not understand, and I knew I had quite a battle ahead of me.

One of the things that helped me was educating myself and my family about bipolar disorder. Jeremy's doctor recommended reading the book *A Brilliant Madness*, by Patty Duke. I had Bob, Jaehnel, and even Jeremy read it. Jaehnel was heartbroken for her brother and was very supportive of him. She was always worried about him. The book was very helpful to all of us and gave me hope. Patty Duke also suffered from bipolar I and she struggled for years with pain and suffering, but she was doing well at the time when she wrote the book. Her symptoms were so similar to Jeremy's.

I began to read voraciously, not only this book but others as well. I read a lot about the genetics of bipolar disorder.

Much of the research done on bipolar disorder indicates that there is a very strong genetic base. However, there are still many studies being done to isolate the gene or genes involved. The condition can skip several generations, or show up in one or two of three children or not all. Two unaffected parents can have a child that is affected, which indicates that one or both are carriers. My daughter Jaehnel may be a carrier, or she might not be.

If Jaehnel was worried that she would develop bipolar, she never said. Both Jaehnel and Elissa have expressed concern about the possibility of their children developing bipolar, but we just hope, pray, and go on. Continued genetic studies are needed for a cure or to eradicate the disease but I am hopeful that they will be found one day, even if it's not in my lifetime.

Even though I wasn't a regular when it came to prayer, I prayed every night asking if I could please have my son back. I tried to bargain with God. I begged and pleaded. I missed Jeremy so much. I insisted that if Jeremy could just come back to me, I would find a way to give back tenfold. I would find a way to help other youth with bipolar disorder for the rest of my life. Amazingly, it seemed that my prayer was actually answered weeks later, as Jeremy was getting better.

At the time, I was working in the social work field for New Jersey Children Services. There was an announcement of two openings for two social workers to work specifically with adolescents. I applied and got one of the positions. As I looked over my new caseload, I saw that several of the young people I would be working with were in residential facilities. Some had been abandoned by their parents, who didn't understand their behavior, and some were failed adoptions. Adoptive parents didn't want them anymore. My new caseload had adolescents, and 80 percent of those were diagnosed with bipolar disorder. I thanked God, and spent the next many years advocating for these kids with a passion that was deeper than anyone knew.

•

Even though lithium is the first-choice medicine for bipolar, it can be dangerous with alcohol consumption, so they put Jeremy on Depakote. The problem with medications for bipolar is that they have to build up a therapeutic level in the blood, which takes about six weeks. So, around the end of May, I started seeing glimpses of my son coming back to us.

Of course, his grades fell quickly with the onset of his diagnosis. With Jeremy's psychiatrist involved, the Child Study Team created a 504 plan. He had a shortened day, a tutor for English, and I tutored him in math during the summer. Amazingly, he caught up enough and graduated on time.

Jeremy needed time to recover, so he worked with his dad in his construction business for a year. Usually it was just the two of them working together. Occasionally, they would hire extra help. Bob was doing all kinds of construction work back then. They became very close, spending almost every day together.

Jeremy's best friend was away at school in Washington state. He was going to come home for the summer and had lots of belongings to bring back with him. He had asked Jeremy to fly out there, spend a week or so with him, and drive back, making a cross-country trip out of it. Jeremy agreed. About two weeks later, I received a call from his best friend calling from a phone booth. He sounded very distraught. He said Jeremy was not doing well and wanted to talk to me. I talked to him and quickly assessed that he was in a manic episode. He sounded like he was crying and said he needed to hear my voice. I asked to speak to his friend again. I asked his friend if he knew if Jeremy was taking his medication, and he said he didn't know. I asked him if Jeremy was doing any of the driving, and he said no. I asked if he thought he could make it home okay, and he said he was going to try. I told him to call us if he couldn't. I felt so bad for both of them. What was supposed to be a great experience of a lifetime turned out terrible. I suspected they had done drugs, but didn't ask because I didn't expect an honest answer. They made it home with the friend driving straight through. Jeremy came home, once again, to recuperate.

His friend transferred to a school in Vermont. They had little contact after that. I could see Jeremy's pain of losing his best friend. Relationships are so hard when you have bipolar disorder.

The next July, Jeremy went to a technical school in Rhode Island for a year to learn mechanics. There was no on-campus housing, so we secured a small apartment for him off campus. I was so afraid to leave him alone in an apartment five hours away. He did well and was getting straight A's, but he missed us so much that he often drove home on weekends. Easter week, 1999, he came home for a visit that threw him into his worst episode yet, detailed in the opening of the book.

Jeremy was better within a few days of returning home, but I really think it resulted in him having PTSD. He tried going back to his apartment, but he just couldn't. He only had about ten days of school left and since he had no absences and excellent grades, they graduated him and awarded him his certificate. He couldn't go back for the graduation. Does this disease have no mercy? It's like living in a nightmare.

Ruth

My family spoke very little of my half-sister Ruth or my mother. Jeremy often asked about them. I knew what he was thinking. Ruth had the same disease, and our family was basically estranged from her. I cringed when people used the words "bipolar" or "crazy" to describe people in a derogatory way. Without Jeremy even asking directly, I would explain to him that their situations were very different. Jeremy had accepted that he had an illness and accepted treatment. It was not in our power to force treatment upon an adult. Only the State of California was able to do that in a court of law.

Years later, I spent some time trying to track Ruth down. She was no longer at the group home. I finally found her at a board and care home, which seemed a lot like a nursing home. I introduced myself as her half-sister who had raised her daughter. The person on the other end of the phone said, "She has a daughter? That's interesting, because she seems to be stuck in thinking that she is constantly in labor, about to give birth." The person advised that Ruth was not at all coherent. I phoned a few more times over the years to check in on her. A different person answered the phone each time with a very similar response. Even though Ruth had gone through years with untreated mental illness, this development still surprised me. I began to research the connection between Alzheimer's, dementia, and bipolar. Ruth was only in her early sixties at the time.

I learned that someone with bipolar does have a greater risk of developing early onset Alzheimer's or dementia, especially if the bipolar disorder is untreated for years. The more episodes the person goes through, the more the disease progresses and there is more damage to the brain. Alzheimer's, dementia, Parkinson's, and bipolar and schizophrenia all have to do with unbalanced levels of dopamine in the brain. It makes me wonder why Alzheimer's, dementia, and Parkinson's do not carry the stigma that bipolar and schizophrenia do.

Treatment

THE NEXT FEW YEARS, Jeremy was relatively stable, although he still suffered some episodes and periods of instability. His doctor changed his medicine from Depakote to lithium. Lithium seemed to be more effective, even though the medical community still seems unsure of how it works. Depakote is an anticonvulsant that stops the brain from over-firing during mania. Lithium is a natural salt element. As the years went by, it seemed like the doctor had to add a medicine for each symptom: an antidepressant for the depression symptoms and an antipsychotic for preventing delusions, hallucinations, and sleep problems. It seemed that Jeremy always had to juggle a cocktail of prescriptions that didn't always agree with each other. Careful monitoring was always necessary to make sure the antidepressants didn't start causing mania and that the lithium levels were therapeutic but not toxic. But I was grateful that Jeremy accepted and understood he had an illness and was compliant and responsive to medication.

I thought about my sister Ruth and how different Jeremy's life and our lives could have been had he been untreated. If Jeremy hadn't accepted his disease, complied with treatment, and didn't have our love and support, he may have very well landed in the homeless population wandering the streets. I think about this every time I see a homeless person.

I once asked the doctor if drug use caused the mental illness or the mental illness caused drug use. He said since Jeremy's first sign of depression was at the age of fourteen and we have the strong genetic factor in our family, it is likely that it would have surfaced either way. After all, there was no drug use involved in either my mother's or my sister's disease. Whether he aggravated it or made it come out sooner, we will never know. He said it's like, "What came first, the chicken or the egg?"

Believe it or not, Jeremy never had problems getting a job. Keeping it was the difficult part. After he graduated from technical school he worked for a few marinas and motorcycle shops as a mechanic. Before long, he would run into a period of instability, especially if the job started to involve stress.

He once worked for a motorcycle shop and was so happy there. His boss said he was the best worker he had ever had. He began to make plans for Jeremy to take over his business, as he eventually wanted to move to North Carolina and get involved in racing. He even planned for Jeremy to move into one of the homes on the same property the shop was on. Jeremy was feeling confident, working long hours, and making good money. He moved into a house with a friend and they shared the rent.

I started to worry about him when I didn't hear from him much. One night, he called me at 9:30 at night from the shop. He was alone, and I said, "Jeremy, what are you doing there at this time of night?" I knew the shop had been closed for hours.

He started crying and said, "I'm organizing my tools and I just can't get them right. I'm not doing well."

My heart broke for him. I said, "Oh Jeremy, just come home."

He said, "What about my job and my house?"

I said, "Don't worry, we'll work it out. Just come home now and rest."

So, he did. I asked him if he was taking his medicine, and he couldn't remember.

During times between jobs, Jeremy usually worked with his dad in construction when he was able. He never got stressed with his dad, and they had a special relationship. Jeremy was always so pleasant, polite, and a hard worker. Bob's customers loved him.

Sometimes friends and even family would comment and insinuate that we shouldn't keep taking Jeremy in and that he would never learn to live on his own. When Jeremy was stable, he presented so well that few people truly understood how serious his illness could be. It was often an invisible illness. I didn't really get insulted or let it bother me. I knew it was something that they didn't understand. Jeremy's family was like his oxygen, and there was no way you could take your child's oxygen away.

Jeremy would often get worse before he got better. Whenever his medicine wasn't right, it would take weeks to bring him back again. These were the times that Jeremy would self- medicate. Substance use was definitely a symptom of his disease, and we could see the connection. During these worrisome times, I would fear that late night phone call. One such night we got a call from the police. He had gotten stopped while driving and been charged with DUI based on the road sobriety test. They said the breathalyzer didn't work so they didn't have a documented level. We suspected that his level was lower than they expected so we didn't think this would hold up in court, but it did. Basically, we had hired a lousy lawyer. Jeremy lost his license for six months.

On and Off Medication

At one point, I believe Jeremy was about twenty-three, he decided that since he was stable now, he could go off his medicine. He and a friend were at a bar in town. His friend called me and was frantic. Jeremy was not making any sense and had fallen down on the sidewalk. They asked him to leave the bar and told him he was not allowed there anymore. Jeremy wanted to drive his own car home and he and the friend got into a physical altercation over taking the car keys away. Bob went down there and was able to bring Jeremy home, but he was not at all rational. We tried to talk him into admitting himself in the hospital to get back to being stabilized on his meds. Jeremy was so bad that we called the police to ask for assistance in getting him to the hospital.

As soon as he knew we called the police, he ran. The police arrived and helped us look for him. It was winter, and it was dark. They woke all our neighbors in the middle of the night to see if he was at their home. Bob and Jeremy's friend found him in their barn, hiding in the hay in a corner. Bob brought him home and the police talked to him and left. They seemed to have forgotten that the reason we called was not that he was missing, but we needed help getting him hospitalized. So once again, we had to get through another episode alone.

At this time, Jeremy was not a willing participant in his recovery. We brought him to his psychiatrist and he told her he refused to go back on medicine. She said that in that case, she would have to drop him as a patient, as he would be too much of a liability. I didn't know what to do, so I finally told him he could no longer stay in our home if he didn't take his medicine. We had taken his driving privileges away and had his car keys. He packed a backpack and got on his bicycle. It was raining, and he was holding an umbrella while trying to ride the bike down the driveway. I watched him and cried. A few minutes later he was back. He was crying too. He said he knew he could never make it on his own and he agreed to take medicine. I hugged him and went to work finding a new psychiatrist.

A couple of years later, after a few years of relative stability, Jeremy had severe pains in his abdomen. He went to our doctor and the doctor sent him immediately for an MRI. He drove himself, and at the MRI they sent him immediately to the hospital. His appendix was about to burst. We got a call from the hospital that he had gone into emergency surgery. When we got to the hospital, he was just waking up and was in a lot of pain. He was placed on a morphine drip and had a few days without his lithium medication, which would lower his levels. This made me very nervous. He came home after a couple of days to recover with a short-term prescription for pain.

Shortly after this event, we received a phone call that woke us up at 2 A.M. It was the police. Jeremy had been stopped and a small package of cocaine was in his pocket. Once again, my husband had to go to the police station. We were shocked. We had no idea that he was using cocaine. The next morning, I couldn't look at him or talk to him. He scheduled an evaluation for himself and got into an intensive outpatient rehab facility. He went every day and went to AA meetings every night. This continued while his court date kept getting delayed. He started to love AA and the support he got there. He did not drink alcohol, smoke marijuana, or do any other drugs for almost a year. This was probably the happiest year of his adult life. He loved to go early to the meetings and make the coffee and bring refreshments. It was his social life. We could see how much better his medicine helped without the interference of beer, pot, or anything else.

The definition of happiness completely changed for me. Every day that Jeremy was okay was a good day, because I knew how bad the bad days could be. It took very little to make me happy. People would often comment how I was always so positive. All it took to make me happy was the health and happiness of my kids.

Unfortunately, all good things come to an end. Jeremy started to tell us about a girl in AA who was flirting with him and wanted to go out with him. He said he was very hesitant because they were not supposed to date for a year. Jeremy was soon approaching a year's time. He was twenty-six years old and I knew he wanted to find someone to love and have a family with some day. I thought, what could be better than dating a girl that was also committed to staying clean and sober? So, I encouraged him to go out with her. Well, I soon learned that not everyone in AA is committed to being clean and sober. She convinced him to stop going to AA. She also convinced him that he shouldn't take his medicine; that he should be himself. Of course, they relapsed together, and I regretted ever encouraging him to date her.

Believe it or not, Jeremy dated two more girls who talked him into going off his medication. They thought he could achieve the same results a more natural way, with vitamins and smoothies. I think Jeremy was at the point of believing that if he did not drink or do any drugs that maybe it was true that he could manage without medication. I wish more people understood this disease. You wouldn't tell someone with diabetes to go off their insulin, or someone with cancer or heart disease to go off of their medicine.

One of his girlfriends was scared away when Jeremy started ducking behind the kitchen table hiding from someone scary that none of the rest of us saw. The other one, who Jeremy was madly in love with, came to a family wedding with us in Vermont. She was scared away when he started telling her that it was so nice that her parents could come to the wedding with us. Her parents were not there. It didn't help that on the ride home he kept telling her he thought one of his friends was trying to kill him.

After Jeremy got back on track with his medicine, he seemed to have learned the two most important lessons in taking care of his illness: 1) to never go off his medicine and 2) to not aggravate his illness with drugs or alcohol. He was more mature now, and we were sure he had won his battle. For the several years that followed he did fairly well, and remained fairly stable. He spoke often about the evils of drugs, and how guilty he felt that he may have made his illness worse. He did a lot of research online and even spoke at times about the possibility of becoming a certified alcohol and drug counselor.

I often imagined what Jeremy's life would have been like without his disease. I'm sure he would have had a tremendous measure of success.

I gleaned the following information from the website Addictionpolicy.org

- Addiction should instead be referred to as substance use disorder. Twenty-one million people in our nation suffer from it. That's one in seven people.

- Substance use disorder began being studied as a brain disorder in the 1950s. In the 1990s, scans began to show how the brain is affected by substance use. It begins destroying tissue function in the prefrontal cortex where decision-making ability lies. That part of the brain is hijacked and the person needs more and more of the drug, the brain tissue becoming increasingly damaged.

- There are risk factors that may contribute to a person's vulnerability to this disease: genetics, age of exposure, environmental factors (such as parental involvement and influence), and drug availability. The adolescent brain, still developing until age twenty-six, is more susceptible to addiction taking hold,

- Brain scans show that a brain suffering from substance use disorder can heal and get better. This is usually a long and difficult process. (Addiction Policy Forum, "What is Addiction?")

- Addiction needs to be treated as the medical condition it is.

- That will happen when those affected can tell their stories and seek help without secret and shame.

The Last Hospitalization

On September 12, 2014, Eric Frein, a thirty-one-year-old, ambushed Pennsylvania Police Barracks, shooting two police officers, killing one, and seriously injuring the other. This was the beginning of a forty-eight-day manhunt through miles of wilderness. There were several reported sightings. Our home is only about ten miles from the Pennsylvania border, and at least one of the suspected sightings was on the New Jersey side.

Around this same time period, Jeremy, who had been doing quite well for a number of years, had decided to stop smoking and asked the doctor for Chantix. After being uncomfortable with the side effects of Chantix, he decided to stop taking it.

One weekend night, he was hanging out at a friend's house. His friend was leaving to see his girlfriend. It was late, and Jeremy was already half asleep on the sofa. His friend told him just to stay on the sofa. The next morning, we received a call from Jeremy at the hospital. He was not making much sense and had me quite confused. He said he was just getting checked out and he would be fine. It wasn't until we spoke with the nurse that the story came together. The nurse was also confused until we told her that Jeremy had bipolar and was recently taking Chantix but stopped abruptly.

She explained that Jeremy was at his friend's house and said he saw Eric Frein in the house. He got up and got the only weapon he had, which was a chain saw. After checking the whole house, the bathroom door was closed and so Jeremy decided that Eric Frein was hiding in the bathroom. He started to saw the bathroom door with the chainsaw. Once he got in, he saw that Eric was not inside. At that point, Jeremy feared for his life and didn't know where Eric was, so he called the police. The Blairstown Township Police came. Jeremy explained the situation to them. They checked the house, not finding anyone. The police talked Jeremy into coming with them to the hospital to be checked out, so he agreed. They brought him there, and he had a psychiatric evaluation.

I am grateful to the Blairstown Police for handling this situation the way they did. I have read many instances where police were not properly trained to handle situations of mental illness and the results were tragic.

The doctor gave Jeremy some Risperdal and called Jeremy's regular psychiatrist. Risperdal has often been helpful in getting Jeremy out of manic episodes.

We picked up Jeremy from the hospital and his regular psychiatrist called. He explained that Chantix can often trigger episodes, especially going off of it suddenly. Memories of the Chantix commercials came back to me, cautioning about risks of someone with mental illness. The doctor prescribed more Risperdal until Jeremy came out of this episode.

Eric Frein was eventually captured on October 30, 2014 and sentenced to death in 2017.

Friends or Foes?

In September, 2016, Jeremy and a friend, Cody, were roasting a pig all day. A mutual friend of theirs was having a big party that night. Jeremy stopped home and said he was going back to the party with Cody and he seemed very excited, saying it should be a lot of fun. Jeremy arrived home the next morning. I asked how the party was and he said he ended up not going. He spent the night at an old friend's house, Calvin.

"Calvin?" I said. "You haven't seen him in about fifteen years now! Where does he live?"

"He lives in Ridge Valley, NY now. I bumped into him and he talked me into coming to his house and staying over."

"Where did you bump into him?" I asked.

"Ummm, I forget."

"You forget? It was just last night!"

I was more than a little worried. The last thing I remembered about Calvin was that he spent time in jail for drugs, although I don't' remember the details.

Jeremy started going to Calvin's more and more. Calvin was divorced and living in his house with his son, Calvin, Jr., or better known as CJ. Calvin was forty-three and CJ was twenty-two. One day, Jeremy announced that he was moving in with Calvin and CJ.

He said, "Mom, I know you think he's not good, but he's becoming my best friend and really helps me. He's so good to talk to and gives me confidence."

At the time, Jeremy was working with his dad in construction, but his dad had had several surgeries and severe arthritis so was not working as much as he used to. Jeremy's plan was for him, Calvin, and CJ to work on jobs together.

I guess this worked out okay for a while, but Jeremy began complaining that he was going through too much money. Calvin and CJ had a past electric bill of over $900, which needed to be paid in order to get the heat and electric turned on. Jeremy was buying a lot of food and contributing more than their initial agreement. I suggested that they were maybe taking advantage of him, but he didn't believe it. He still considered them his best friends.

Jeremy started spending a lot of weekends at home, and a lot of his things went missing while he was gone. Calvin and CJ claimed that their shed was burglarized and that's what happened to his missing belongings. Even Jeremy started to question whether he could trust them, but would always come back to the thinking that they were his best friends and wouldn't do that. Jeremy was so vulnerable and trusting. Too trusting.

One day Calvin came to our house with Jeremy. While Jeremy was getting some of his things together, Calvin and I spoke in the kitchen. Calvin kept saying how he was really trying to help Jeremy and talk to him a lot. Jeremy told him that he worried that he was drinking too much beer and wanted to stop so Calvin was trying to help him with that. He said, "I don't drink, not a drop. Nothing. Completely sober." I felt like he was trying to win me over. I feel like I'm pretty intuitive when it comes to people, and I wasn't getting a good feeling at all.

Jeremy lived with them for about three or four months and then seemed to have a moment of clarity. He came home one day and said he didn't belong there. "They're not my kind of people." Needless to say, we agreed and encouraged him to move all his belongings back home, which he did.

I was initially so happy about this decision, but apparently there was a draw there that he could not resist. He began spending weekends there. Then going there several nights during the week. Sometimes he would leave 7:00 at night and return at 10:00 so he could get up for work the next day. It was over an hour ride there, one way. The subject was one of contention between us. Jeremy would claim he was just going for company. He needed some sort of social life. He needed to see friends. He still had friends in our area but most were married and had kids. I wondered how much time he could actually spend visiting when he had almost three hours of driving.

I reminded myself that he was thirty-nine years old. Emotionally, though, he was not thirty-nine. Jeremy looked and acted more like a twenty-one-year-old. The adult male brain is not fully developed until about the age of twenty-six. When a mental illness develops, the brain slows or stops in development. Jeremy did not have the emotional maturity of a thirty-nine-year-old, which is why I often found myself treating him and worrying about him like an eighteen- to twenty-year-old.

Bob and I had been spending a couple of months in Florida every winter and spring since I retired from my full-time job in 2011. In 2017, we were scheduled to be there through March and April. I was watching my littlest grandson every day, and picking up the older boys at the bus stop at 3:30. Jaehnel had been seeking alternate babysitting plans each time we went to Florida. This year she asked Jeremy if he wanted to do it, and he said he did. He would stay in our house and take care of it, too. Since he was working with his dad, being his nephews' nanny would be perfect for him while we were gone. He had such a great relationship with his nephews, and he truly enjoyed time with them.

Jaehnel expressed concern while we were in Florida that he was continuing the strange behavior of driving to New York several nights a week. He often asked his sister for money when in reality he should have had plenty. He was working, and he had recently sold his truck, a four-wheeler, and two wood stoves.

About two weeks before we came home from Florida, Jeremy called and told us that he would be working with Kenny in his landscaping business. This landscaping business used to be my son-in-law's, and he had passed it on to his brother, who was good friends with Jeremy. Jeremy was so excited. He felt as though it was a family business that he would be part of. We were happy, but Bob expressed some concern. It was getting warm in New Jersey and would be getting even warmer. Having had plenty of experience working outdoors with Jeremy, his dad doubted he could work the hours that this job demanded in the heat while taking lithium. Lithium has side effects of dehydration, thirst, and lethargy, especially in the heat.

We came home in early May, and Jeremy had started working with Kenny. They were working twelve hours a day sometimes, and Jeremy was still making frequent visits to New York. Jeremy said he was doing great, and Kenny agreed. He was still full of energy and not sleeping much at night. We warned him that he needed to take care of himself so he didn't throw himself into an episode. He was losing weight and his confidence was up.

We were puzzled. I was cautiously happy for Jeremy, but still wondered what was going on. He didn't usually have this much energy on lithium, and he could be heading for the manic side.

On Mother's Day, Jeremy gave me a card and the words he wrote just seemed to scream at me. Oh, he always got me a card, but usually just signed it "Love, Jeremy." This time he wrote, "I love you so much. You mean so much to me." He also hugged me one day and said, "Don't worry, Mom, I'm not drinking at all or smoking pot. I would never do that. I know it's not good for me." He often said, "Do you need a hug?" but I often wondered if it was really him that needed one. He would hug me and say, "Mom, you're the best." Then I started to say it to him when I hugged him. We were so close. I loved him so much. He would often say that he didn't think he was going to live past the age of forty and I would get so upset with him, saying, "Don't say that! Why are you saying that?" He said he had learned that people with bipolar have a shorter life span for several reasons, including links to heart disease, risky behavior, suicide, and detrimental effects on organs from a lifetime of medications.

Anguish

It was Friday, June 2, 2017. Jeremy came home from work and was outside smoking a cigarette. He didn't look good.

I asked, "Jeremy are you okay? You don't seem like yourself lately. Are you taking your medicine?"

"Yes, I am. You're right though, I feel a little jittery. I think maybe my anti-depressant dosage is too high and I should see the doctor about adjusting it." He was able to convince me this could have been true.

He got ready to go to Calvin and CJ's. They had recently moved into a motel. When Calvin's ex-wife had left him a couple of years ago, he stayed in the house, but it eventually foreclosed and they had to get out in May. Jeremy came home that night. He hadn't been sleeping over there because he no longer had his own room and bed. Calvin and CJ only had two beds in the hotel.

He woke up Saturday morning and said, "Well, I guess we're going to the shore tomorrow."

"The shore?" I said. "It's going to be sixty-five degrees and cloudy. Why would you go to the shore?"

"Oh, just something to do."

I immediately became worried. Jeremy didn't even seem like he wanted to go. I knew the plan originated from Calvin and CJ. Of course, Jeremy was going to be doing the driving and taking his car.

Jeremy was so vulnerable and had such a hard time saying no to anyone. He was the kind of person that selfish people with their own agenda could use, prey on, and take advantage of.

Saturday, he was smoking outside in the garage. I asked Bob to go talk to him. "I just have such a bad feeling about this. Jeremy doesn't seem like himself. Please talk him out of going. I just know something terrible is going to happen."

Bob went out there briefly and talked to Jeremy. He came in and said, "You have to leave him alone. He's an adult."

I knew he was repeating Jeremy's sentiments about my concern. Jeremy also mentioned to his dad that maybe he wasn't himself and was taking too many anti-depressants. He agreed to make a doctor's appointment to see about adjusting his medicines.

When someone has bipolar, it is often difficult to determine if it is the bipolar or a drug influence that is changing their behavior. Both affect the same chemicals in the brain.

Sunday morning, Jeremy got up and got ready. He said, "Yup, going to the shore. Got $400 in my wallet."

"$400! Why are you bringing so much money? You won't need that much money." I thought it was strange that he mentioned this, almost a cry for help. So once again, I tried to help by talking him out of going, but he didn't accept the help, said goodbye, and left.

Later, on Sunday, I texted him to see if everything was okay. He answered, but told me his phone was almost dead and he forgot his charger so of course I didn't expect to hear from him anymore that day. At 1:20 A.M., I got a text from him that said he was staying over at Calvin and CJ's. He said he was too tired to drive home and he would be getting up early the next morning to make it to work. Calvin had to get up early for work too.

The next morning, he didn't come home so I assumed he went right to work from Calvin's. I went about my day's activities, which that day involved watching my little two-and-a-half-year-old grandson while his mom worked. I picked up my two older grandsons at the bus stop at 3:30 as usual. I got home around 4:30, and shortly after, received a phone call from my daughter, Jaehnel. Her brother-in-law Kenny had called her.

"Why didn't Jeremy show up for work today?" Jaehnel asked me.

"He didn't show up for work?"

Immediately, Jaehnel started to say she knew something was wrong. She said Kenny waited a half hour for him. That's just not like Jeremy to not even call or anything. She had been trying to text and call him with no response. I tried to think positively, and said maybe his phone was dead, but truly, I was just as worried. The next half hour we were both texting and calling Jeremy's phone and Calvin's phone with no response.

The phone rang. It was a New York phone number. The caller introduced himself as Detective Barone and asked me several questions: name, relation to Jeremy, when was the last time I talked to and saw Jeremy, where did I think Jeremy was at this time. I told him I thought he was at his friend Calvin's. I feared that Jeremy had gotten in some kind of trouble and that he had gotten my phone number from Jeremy. He explained that he had Jeremy's phone and had just read the text from me that said "Is everything okay?" He had gotten my phone number from the text.

Then the most painful words I ever had to hear: "I am a detective in the coroner's office in Ridge Valley, NY. I'm so sorry to inform you that your son has passed away."

I thought it must be some mistake but he said, "Yes, I am so sorry. Usually we send the local police out to inform you, and they are probably on their way, but I feel in this circumstance, I had to tell you."

In my state of shock, I asked what happened.

He advised that there was a current investigation, and that Calvin and CJ were being questioned extensively. He continued that Jeremy had left the hotel room to go home but came back about twenty minutes later saying he didn't feel good and he thought he should stay over. Calvin and CJ said they gave him some blankets and made him comfortable on the floor. The next morning Calvin got up early to go to work but assumed Jeremy changed his mind about going to work and decided to sleep in. When Calvin got home from work at 4:00 he saw Jeremy was still sleeping and tried to wake him. Apparently, CJ was sleeping all day in the bed next to him. When Calvin realized he was not sleeping, he tried to give him CPR but it was too late. Jeremy was expired and Calvin called 911.

Detective Barone said he knew I was in shock and told me to take his number. He would call me the next day. There would be an autopsy, which is standard with any sudden death.

I had to tell Bob, but it wasn't even real to me. We cried together. I got a frantic phone call from Jaehnel asking if I heard anything. I wish that I could have told her in person, but I was crying and if I told her I needed to tell her something in person she would have known. I didn't think my heart could tear anymore, but when I heard her screams of horror my heart just ripped some more for both my children, one gone and the other in so much pain.

Jaehnel came over, we cried and hugged and cried some more. I didn't have the strength to talk to anyone so I called my sister, Christa, and asked her to tell the family. Bob called one of his brothers and asked him to tell his side of the family. Elissa came over. She was very much a sister to both my kids. We cried and hugged some more. I was completely unable to talk to anyone on the phone. I couldn't even get through a sentence.

Arrangements

THE NEXT DAY Detective Barone called back. He had done the autopsy and said that Jeremy had an enlarged heart. This could be caused by many things: smoking, alcohol, high blood pressure, genetics, drug use. He said that they would know more when toxicology reports come back but that this could take a couple of months. He did say that they found something of a white residue in Jeremy's possession. Detective Barone's job was to conduct an investigation into the cause of death only. He explained that there would be another investigation conducted by the police department, and he gave me their name and phone number. He told me I would immediately have to decide on funeral arrangements and let him know about the transportation of Jeremy's body.

There is definitely something numbing about the death of a loved one. Especially when it is a son or daughter and it is so unexpected. It's not supposed to happen. It defies the laws of nature. I think the numbness is a way of the body, heart, and soul protecting itself. It actually helps you get through the horror of planning your child's funeral, and greeting and hosting all those family and friends. I remember I felt like I was going through the motions but I wasn't really there. I was in a fog—a fog of grief.

As many of our family and friends in Florida, North Carolina, and Delaware began to make travel arrangements, Jaehnel, Bob, and I met with the funeral director in town to plan Jeremy's funeral. What would he have wanted? I never got the chance to ask him, thinking this event was nowhere near. The director asked us basic questions to be included in Jeremy's obituary. His obituary turned out to be very generic, and afterwards I was upset with myself because there were so many wonderful things I could have said in his obituary, but I couldn't even think. I was still numb. I couldn't eat, either. I didn't feel hunger and I didn't enjoy food. I didn't enjoy anything. I had to remind myself that I had to eat to survive.

We decided on cremation and a three-hour visitation period at the funeral home the following Sunday. Elissa graciously offered to host the repast after the visitation, seeing that I was in no condition to do it.

It was Thursday, the eighth of June. Jaehnel and I were quietly sitting on my deck. She told me that she thought Jeremy died at around 4:20 A.M. She said in that early morning on the fifth, she had woken up in a panic attack and was sweating. She looked at the clock on her nightstand and it said 4:20. She'd never had panic attacks before. I believe she's probably right. The two of them were so connected. Best buddies for life and afterward.

As we were talking, a beautiful black and blue butterfly came and was flying around us. At first, we didn't think anything of it except that it was a beautiful butterfly. It ended up hovering around us for hours. Jaehnel said, "Did you know that the butterfly is a symbol of the afterlife, when your soul leaves your body? It also means that you will be more powerful in the afterlife than life on earth. I bet Jeremy was cremated today."

The Funeral

We were overwhelmed with the love and support of our family and friends at the funeral home. Close to three hundred people came to visit and say goodbye to Jeremy. Everyone who knew and loved Jeremy and our family came, except for the two people that Jeremy considered his best friends. Calvin and CJ weren't there. The first few days I tried calling them and texting them. I wanted more answers, but they didn't respond. It was Sunday, June 11. It was a hot day, in the 90s, and people waited on a line that went outside the funeral home for hours. Our family greeted everyone on the line for the entire visitation time.

I could feel the love and compassion through the hugs and the tears. My heart could feel the sincerity. All the people who came either loved Jeremy, loved us, or both. So many of Jeremy's friends that he grew up with came, and I realized that so many of them had seen Jeremy through an episode of his illness but they still loved him. I realized how Jeremy had already changed the face of bipolar and mental illness for so many.

A couple of days before, my sister Christa, her daughter Erika, Elissa, her daughter Paige, Jaehnel and I had come together at my house to go through pictures. We made poster boards of pictures with Jeremy in them to have on display at the funeral home. Jeremy was so handsome. Bluish, green eyes with long lashes and thick curly hair—Very blonde when he was little but a darker blonde when he got older. He usually had his hair cut very short, and I would tell him he should grow it out a little to show off those beautiful curls. He was stocky and strong, only about 5'8" tall. His medicines would often make him gain weight, which is one of the things he didn't like about them.

One of the larger pictures fell down during the visitation hours and my son-in-law, Kevin, picked it up and put it up again only for it to fall down again two more times. Jaehnel's friend, Melissa said, "Do you know that's a sign that he's here?" I had never heard of that before.

I didn't give it much thought. I hadn't thought about spiritual visits since our honeymoon cabin. When I lost my father, I had a dream that he and I were talking on the phone. I could hear him but he couldn't hear me. I thought it was nothing but a dream. I never thought for a second that it might be a spiritual visit.

At the end of the visitation hours, we had set aside a time for a eulogy and for anyone who wanted to speak. I decided it was a chance for me to say all the beautiful things I should have said about Jeremy in his obituary, but I was too numb and in shock to think. After all, I thought, no one knew Jeremy like I did. After I thanked everyone for their overwhelming support, I began:

I wasn't sure if I could do this but then I thought, "I have to, I am his mom." Jeremy, my dear sweet beautiful baby, and oh, how he was! Even the nurses secretly told me he was the most beautiful baby in the nursery; and so, he grew to be beautiful in the inside as well. He was such a happy child. He loved life, people, and especially his family. He made us laugh all the time.

Later, when his disease surfaced, he had his demons and life became a struggle but he continued to be the good, loving person that he was. There were times I thought he had won the battle.

He loved the outdoors, camping, his ATVs and motorcycles, animals, kids . . . especially his nephews. He loved them so. He would do anything for anybody and never had a bad word to say about anyone. Isn't it funny how some people don't realize they're special at all? They are thoughtful without even thinking about it.

I hope he is looking down and able to see this outpouring of love. You, our family, friends, and Jeremy's friends are helping us make it through this. So many of you came from so far away. We appreciate so much every way you have reached out to us whether it was cards, bringing food, flowers, hugs, calls, helping with pictures, condolences, words of comfort, being here today. It helps our hearts to know that so many knew his goodness and kindness. We couldn't have made it this far without you.

Isn't it lovely how special people can teach us so much about living? Let Jeremy's life be a source of hope and inspire us. Be kind to one another, don't stigmatize, stay as mentally and physically well as we can and help others to do so.

Whenever Jeremy hugged me, he said, "You're the best." It got to be where I would try to beat him to it and say, "You're the best" before he did. He will live on in our hearts forever. Grief can never take away the happiness and memories we've shared.

•

A few other people stood up and spoke, but when my brother-in-law, Bo, spoke about how Jeremy saw the good in everyone and was so generous with his time, it touched me. This was true. Jeremy often watched his nephews for his sister and fixed things for people. He didn't mind sharing what came easy to him with people who didn't have the same skills. This reminded me of how Jeremy used to call the two poles of his illness "the good Jeremy and the bad Jeremy," but I used to call it "the well Jeremy and the ill Jeremy."

We had company for a few days but then everyone went home and back to their own lives. We went into our ever-changing new life, trying to find our new normal.

Grief

SOME OF THE STAGES OF GRIEF are said to be shock and denial, pain and guilt, anger, bargaining or blame, depression, acceptance, hope and healing. These stages are different for everyone. For some they are not "stages," but feelings that come and go for varied lengths of time. I continue to experience all of the stages time and time again and they are not linear..Men grieve differently than women, and children grieve differently than adults.

Jeremy often stated that even though he would have loved to have kids, he wouldn't because of the risk of passing on his illness—and he would never want to pass that on to anyone. It would make me sad when he said this. He would always add that he didn't need to have children because he had his nephews and they looked just like him. (They did have quite a resemblance, especially from when Jeremy was a baby.) Jeremy had an amazing relationship with his nephews. They loved him and he loved them so much. He often cared for them when needed.

My little grandsons had tears throughout most of the funeral. The older two were nine years old and knew their buddy was gone. The little one, who was two and a half, was confused for sure. His Uncle Jeremy had given him a huge stuffed dog he named Phoofy. To this day, when he's upset, he needs Phoofy nearby to comfort him. If Kolty's having a bad day, we have to bring Phoofy wherever we go.

Shock and Denial

When it comes to losing a daughter or a son, the shock and denial last a long time. For me it was the whole first year. I would wake up each morning in tears to face the realization that my son was gone, each time still hoping it wasn't true and I was in the middle of some kind of nightmare.

Pain and Guilt

The pain is intense and never goes away. At some point I realized I needed to get used to it and carry it with me the rest of my days but it takes a long time, probably forever.

Guilt is something that accompanies any parent who loses a child, no matter at what age. We start imagining things that we may have done differently that may have changed the course of things. You can go through a million scenarios, but you can't change the end result.

Anger, Bargaining, or Blame

For me, at least, bargaining only found its place in these stages when someone was sick or dying. When Jeremy was diagnosed and ill, I did quite a lot of bargaining with God, but once your loved one is gone and you are grieving their death, there is not much bargaining left to do.

Anger and blame are another story and can stay with you for a long time, maybe forever. My husband and I both experienced anger and blame. I got angry at Bob for not convincing Jeremy to stay home that weekend when I begged him to. I got angry at him for minimizing those first times that Jeremy smoked pot.

I got angry at Calvin and CJ after their lack of response, and lack of answers and explanations. When their stories were inconsistent, I was suspicious of their involvement. I was angry that they were the last ones with Jeremy and that 911 wasn't called for fifteen hours. I asked each one of them what happened to Jeremy and what the white powder they found on him was. Calvin's explanation was that Jeremy stole his dad's pain pills after his dad had surgery and he got addicted to heroin. I know this wasn't true. The way they prescribe those pills, his dad would have noticed if even one was missing. They are counted to the day, and his dad was in so much pain, I know he couldn't have spared any. When Calvin talked to the police, however, he told them that he knew Jeremy had done cocaine but he didn't know of him ever doing heroin. CJ's explanation was that he never knew of any white powder. He pointed the finger at one of Jeremy's friends in our town who Jeremy grew up with. The inconsistencies of their stories raised my suspicion.

I later messaged Calvin and said, "I wish Jeremy never reconnected with you, he would still be with us today!" Calvin told me to never call or message him again.

I was angry at the police department. It was an open investigation, but they didn't seem to be doing anything to investigate. I called the detective each week to ask for an update. I reminded him that both Calvin and CJ's stories were so inconsistent that they must be hiding something. He agreed but said they don't have any proof. He kept reminding me that they have immunity because they called 911. I insisted that they must have had something to do with either providing the drugs or being a connection. I studied Jeremy's phone bill, and the weekend that he died, there were no unknown phone numbers on his phone bill. Only Calvin's and CJ's.

Several weeks after Jeremy's death, I received a call from the coroner's office with the results of Jeremy's toxicology report. The amounts of milligrams didn't mean anything to me, but I was amazed at what was in his system: cocaine, morphine, fentanyl, and three drugs that were prescribed to him. I wasn't sure if the doctor had directed him to be taking them all at the same time. They were Lamictal, Lexapro, and Seroquel. Lamictal is a mood stabilizer more effective for depression symptoms, and Lexapro is an antidepressant. Seroquel is an antipsychotic. There was also Levamisole, which I had never heard of. I looked it up and found that it is an animal de-wormer. Someone had definitely provided Jeremy with something heavily laced.

I cried on the phone. The detective said that what probably killed him was the fentanyl. They were seeing an increasing number of deaths with fentanyl in the toxicology. He told me that he didn't think Jeremy suffered. He thought he probably fell asleep and never woke up. I knew he didn't know that for sure, and I knew he was trying to make me feel better. I wonder if he sugarcoated it any way he could, whenever he could, for loved ones.

There was no alcohol or marijuana in Jeremy's system. The most surprising was that there was no lithium in his system. Oh, how could he stop taking his lithium? Lithium was what kept him well, what kept the demons away and kept him rational.

I remembered that when I asked CJ what happened that night, he said Jeremy had a couple of beers, a joint, and took his lithium. These three things were not in his system at all—proof of his lying. With all that was in his system, the thought of suicide crossed my mind. After all, there is a large percentage of suicide victims with bipolar disorder, and lithium reportedly helps with preventing suicide. I know many people initially assumed that Jeremy died by suicide because many people knew that he had bipolar. Instead of flowers, I had requested donations the National Association for Mental Illness (NAMI).

A couple of weeks later I got a bill in the mail for Jeremy from his psychiatrist's office. It was for missing his June appointment without canceling. It occurred to me that I had not contacted them. I had called everyone I could think of: his health insurance, car insurance, credit card, etc. But I had not called his psychiatrist's office. I picked up the phone to call. The receptionist answered. I hated making these calls. The words would always spill out with tears and my breath would be taken away, barely able to complete my sentences.

"I received a bill," I said. "The reason Jeremy didn't make his appointment is because he passed away on June 5."

"Oh my God," said the receptionist. "That can't be true. He always did so well. We always used to say how he was our most successful patient. He was so friendly and happy. What happened?"

I told her we'd just learned that he had stopped taking his lithium and had other drugs in his system. She continued her pronouncements of disbelief and I think maybe she was crying too.

After I hung up I thought about how Jeremy used to tell me about the receptionist at the psychiatrist's office. "She's really pretty, a little heavy but really pretty, and she's always nice to me." I remember him saying he asked her out once. "Aww," she said. "I'm flattered, but I have a boyfriend."

A few weeks later, I contacted Jeremy's psychiatrist asking if Jeremy had gone off his lithium with her blessing, or if it was a decision he made on his own. I also wanted to know what other medicines he was supposed to be taking. Of course, she didn't answer me. With the current Health Insurance Portability and Accountability Act (HIPPA) laws,

I didn't think she would. I'm sure she also feared liability and that I would seek legal recourse.

With all that was in Jeremy's system, I still sometimes wonder if he ended his life purposely. I don't think so. Despite his struggles, he loved and enjoyed his family, especially his nephews. I suppose I'll never really know for certain, but one thing I know for sure is that without his lithium, he wasn't in his right mind.

I started to read and research more on the opioid and fentanyl crisis. I learned that China is shipping fentanyl and fentanyl analogs to the US, Canada and Mexico and are not cracking down on illegal factories like they promised to do but are actually giving incentives for production. I know several federal organizations are working together to decrease the illegal drug supply and they do make progress. Despite this, young people continue to die every day.

(Ben Westoff 2019)

In NJ 87 percent of the drug supply is fentanyl. In 2015 it was only 2 percent. Now anyone that takes an illegal drug has only about 13 percent survival rate. (DrugfreeNJ.org, Knock Out Opioid Abuse, Drug Monitoring Initiative, 2020)

I wish there was more we could do to put pressure on China to stop the illegal manufacturing where it originates. China leaders express that the problem is addiction and the US needs to get a handle on it. They seem to not have developed the consideration of substance use disorder as a disease. Maybe the lives of people that have the vulnerability of mental illness including substance use disorder don't matter to some. They matter to us and all the other parents and family members who lost these beautiful young people. I was so angry at every drug dealer and I wanted to find the one that supplied the fentanyl-laced drug to my son. Now I felt like my son was murdered.

I called the detective and told him we had to find the source.

He said, "What do you hope to glean from this?" I think he thought I was seeking revenge.

I said, "What? I don't want anyone else to die!"

I think I hit a nerve then because he said, "Okay, we will try because we both want the same things."

But my calls continued until he stopped taking them. I know he works in an area that is riddled with drugs. I know he was busy, but I felt like he didn't care about my son. Many people look at addiction as a choice, not a disease. The first use may be a choice, but that choice is not to become addicted, to suffer, to change into a completely different person, to lose loved ones, or to die. As much as it scares us, we know that teens and young adults experiment and take chances.

At one point, the detective from the investigating police department said, "No one forced it up his nose." There is less empathy and understanding for people who suffer from substance use disorder and mental illness. When someone dies from lung cancer, we don't say it was their choice because they smoked cigarettes for years. We don't blame someone that dies of a heart attack for not eating right, not exercising, or drinking too much alcohol. These deaths don't carry the same stigma. They didn't choose to die from a heart attack or lung cancer, although maybe the choices they made had a part in it. People don't choose to die because of their addiction either. Substance use disorder is the only disease that is considered a choice.

I sent in a report via a tip line to the Drug Enforcement Administration (DEA), never really expecting to hear back from them. I was shocked when Detective Cooper from the DEA called me one day and wanted to look into Jeremy's case. I told him the whole story and he gave me hope. He cared. I cried on the phone to him while I told my story—Jeremy's story. He said he would contact the detective at the police department and get a report from them. He wanted to talk to Calvin and CJ again but found that they were both in jail for robbery. I thought about the kind of people Jeremy was drawn to when he wasn't stable. His judgment of character was so off.

I called the detective at the Ridge Valley police department and asked him why he didn't report this case to the DEA, especially since he didn't seem to have time to investigate it himself. He said it didn't fall into an appropriate case for the DEA. I was so angry again. I said, "What? My son died from a drug that was laced with fentanyl that kills thousands of people and this wasn't appropriate for the DEA? Why then did the DEA take the case?" The detective just kept reminding me that we had no proof that Calvin and CJ were involved and we had no other leads. He stopped taking my calls until he closed the case.

I told Detective Cooper from the DEA what the police officer said and asked if it was true, that the case wouldn't fall into the category to report to DEA. He said that wasn't true, that actually, anyone can report a tip to the DEA and they get many reports from police departments. How sad, I thought, that thousands of young people are dying from a problem that we can't get under control and agencies aren't working together to do everything they can to end this tragedy of mass destruction.

Detective Cooper tried very hard. He did go out and re-interview Calvin and CJ. He said they cooperated and said they knew about the cocaine but didn't know about any heroin. The detective said that it would be impossible to find the source because you can go on any street corner and buy anything. We first assumed that Jeremy had taken cocaine laced with fentanyl, but the Detective Cooper explained that we couldn't know that because Jeremy had both cocaine and fentanyl in his system, but he could have taken the cocaine earlier. Sometimes heroin is sold that is 100 percent fentanyl. How can anyone be so heartless to know someone would be ingesting something that will likely kill them? It is a cruel world. I had to accept that there will always be unanswered questions about Jeremy's death.

I got angry at Jeremy, too. Bob and I both did. We thought, "How could he do this and hurt all of us and make us suffer and hurt like this?" When Bob would feel this way, I would remind him that Jeremy didn't mean to do this. When I was feeling this way, I shared with my support group. My friend Teresa, who lost her son when he was sixteen, said, "I was angry at Zack sometimes too, but my therapist told me that you can't be angry at someone for something that is not in their control, and I think this was something that was out of Jeremy's control." She was right.

So, the anger and blame went around and around, never really finding a settling place.

Depression

I have suffered depression before and grief really is a type of depression. When there is an untimely death like that of a son or a daughter, depression takes hold and never seems to leave. It is hard to muster every ounce of energy to accomplish the smallest task. My heart ached; my tears flowed. There was a huge hole in my heart that would never be filled. My doctor kept suggesting an increase in depression medication. I kept saying, "But it's grief, not depression." They said that it would help me function better and not cry so much. I finally gave in and it did help me function better, but that ache and longing will stay forever.

Acceptance

I don't think I will ever reach a stage of acceptance. When someone gives you a gift, you happily accept it. When you get a new job, an offer, an invitation, you happily accept it. Acceptance just does not seem like the right word. I will never "happily" accept the loss of my beautiful boy.

I think about the unfulfilled dreams. I had dreams for Jeremy. I hoped that he would find a soulmate to share the rest of his life with and have some children that I could be a grandparent to. Jeremy did well for so many years that I was actually thinking that this dream had a chance of becoming realized. I know deep down inside it was Jeremy's dream too, but with bipolar it is hard to stay in a long-term relationship. If you tell the person about your illness in the beginning, it scares them away. If they find out about it later, it not only scares them away but they feel they have been lied to. Jeremy said he would never have children because of the risk of passing on the disease. I would always argue that we were always so happy to have him, but I realize my point of view was coming from a completely different place. He would say that he would never want a child that had to experience this disease. This made me sad. I know he would have loved to have children. Watching him with his nephews and his girlfriends, I know he would have been a great husband and father.

Hope and Healing

First of all, let me say that in the case of losing a child, healing does not mean that you will ever be the person you were before your loss. Healing just means getting to a place where you can function: finding your "new normal." You are forever changed. Such an important piece of you is gone. You have to reconstruct the pieces of your life the best that you can.

After we received the toxicology results, Bob and I talked about whether we should tell people about Jeremy's cause of death. Bob didn't want to. He said, "Jeremy didn't even want us to know, so he wouldn't want others to know. He'll receive labels that he doesn't deserve. The underlying cause was his mental illness, and people don't understand it."

I wasn't sure if I agreed. I thought about those words, "Jeremy didn't want anyone to know . . . his mental illness . . . people don't understand it." I kept reading about people dying from fentanyl and realized they weren't aware of the risk. I started to feel I should shout it from the rooftops. Stigma and shame are how we got to this place in society. I didn't want to be part of the problem; I wanted to be part of the solution. Keeping things hidden expends a lot of energy—energy that can be useful in other ways.

A Healing Visit

One of the first people I told about the cause of Jeremy's death, outside of the family, was my daughter Jaehnel's ex-boyfriend, Anthony. They dated in high school when Jaehnel was between the ages of fifteen and eighteen. He was at our home for dinner several nights a week and we loved him. He was part of our family. He went camping with us to Lake George Islands, and he and Jeremy shared a tent. I always assumed Jaehnel and Anthony would get married, but once Jaehnel went away to college, they broke up. We were heartbroken, and I always hoped they might get back together, but they didn't. We stayed in touch with Anthony on and off. When Jeremy died, he adopted a manatee for us and we got the paperwork and a T-shirt in the mail. Lose a life; save a life. I tried to call him, text him, and Facebook message him several times to thank him. He was living in the state of Washington. I never got a response. I thought maybe I had the wrong number, so I contacted his sister. The number she gave me was the same one I had.

One day, out of the blue, I received a phone call from Anthony. "Renate, this is Anthony. I'm up at the Glen and I wondered if I could stop by."

"The Glen? That's just a few minutes from my house!"

"Yes, I'm here visiting and I'm on my way back from Philadelphia to Brooklyn. I stopped here for a hike and hopefully to visit you."

When Anthony was part of our family, we hiked at the Glen quite often. The Glen was a beautiful spot with hiking trails, waterfalls, and large pools of water. You could smell the pines when you hiked back there. Anthony hiked there many times with Jaehnel and Jeremy. Some kids would dive from the cliffs into the large pools of water and some got hurt. Ambulances could not get back there so it took the EMTs a long time to get to the injured. I always warned my kids not to jump off the rocks.

"Can I take you to lunch?" Anthony asked.

"Why don't you just come here? Just let me get out of my pajamas." I hadn't seen Anthony in a long time, and considering our recent loss, I knew the visit would be filled with my tears. I didn't want to be out of control in a restaurant. This was a constant concern during this part of my life—breaking down in public. I was even afraid to go grocery shopping.

Anthony said, "Okay, I just really want to hug you."

Anthony arrived at the front door and immediately hugged me and I burst into tears. We had bagels and talked for hours. Our home was not exactly on the way from Philadelphia to Brooklyn, so I was honored by Anthony's visit.

I told him how many times I tried to reach him to thank him for the adopted manatee, but I was never successful.

He said, "I got the messages. I couldn't . . . I just couldn't."

I told him the whole story about Jeremy while my tears flowed. We caught up on his life as well. He told me how much our family meant to him and how much we impacted and influenced his life. Anthony decided to go into environmental studies after our trip to Lake George Islands. He said our family had so much to do with shaping his life and who he is today. I was flattered, but I told him I thought he was giving us too much credit. When he left, I said, "Anthony, you will always hold a place in my heart. I love you."

Still Here

BEFORE JEREMY DIED, Bob started a landscaping project in our yard. He had a huge load of dirt delivered and was about to rent a tractor to spread it. On the fifth of June, everything in our life came to a halt, including the landscaping project.

Three weeks after Jeremy died, on a Monday morning, Bob decided to get back to work and rented a tractor to spread the dirt. I was on my way to the surrogate's office to sign the papers that would make me the administrator of Jeremy's estate. "Estate" sounded like such a ridiculous term for his small list of assets: his car, a motorcycle, and a checking account with about $500. The amount left in his checking account was a shock since he had recently sold a truck and a four-wheeler and was making good money working steadily. I suppose he either spent a lot of money on drugs, his so-called "friends," or both.

I was on my way home from the surrogate's office and stopped at the park where Jaehnel was with her two boys. She had just started her summer vacation from teaching. When we left the park, I asked her if she wanted to come over and she agreed. When I pulled in the driveway, I saw Bob on the tractor spreading the dirt. Jaehnel pulled in behind me, and when she got out, she asked, "Did you or Dad tell Kolton that Dad was renting the tractor today?"

"No," I said. "Dad just made the decision this morning."

Jaehnel said that two-and-a-half-year-old Kolton had said in the car, "I can't wait to go to Momma and Poppa's house and see Poppa on the tractor. It's a cool red tractor."

We tried to figure out how he knew this, but we knew that Jeremy must have told him. It was the only answer, and it was exactly like Jeremy would tell him: "It's a cool tractor."

I had read that young children are sometimes much more connected to the spiritual world. Their minds are not as cluttered and they are open to all without predetermined fears or opinions.

On the fifteenth of July, we babysat our grandsons while Jaehnel and Kevin went to a truck raffle event on the Delaware River. They have it every year and Jaehnel and Kevin go every year. The tickets are expensive, but include food and drinks, music, fireworks, and a huge raffle with unbelievable prizes. The grand prize is a brand-new truck. Every tenth number they pull wins something and the last number pulled wins the truck.

Jaehnel and Kevin came home that night around 1 A.M. and said, "We won, we won!"

We immediately thought they were joking and said, "Yeah, sure." They had to show us pictures of them in front of the truck before we believed them. Then they told us the whole story. There were two tickets left in the barrel. The guy that was pulling the numbers said he put his hand in and one ticket was stuck on the side of the barrel and one was loose. He said something was telling him that he should pick the one that was stuck. It was probably stuck on the side the whole time and was meant to win. Well, he picked it and it was Kevin and Jaehnel's number. Kevin and Jaehnel felt that Jeremy had definitely had a hand in making their ticket stick. Jeremy would be so excited that they won a truck. Motors were his thing.

On July 20, only six weeks after our loss of Jeremy, I had a doctor's appointment. I had been seeing the same doctor for over thirty years. She was a little younger than me and had become almost like a friend. She knew me and she knew my family. I had cried many times in her arms during times Jeremy was not doing well. She prescribed antidepressants during the times I could barely function because I was so worried about him. She came to the funeral.

As soon as she came in the room I burst into tears, and she held me. She tried to comfort me by saying things like, "His suffering is over. He's in a better place."

I said, "I think he would rather be here with us."

Then she asked me if I had had any signs from him.

I said yes. Besides Jaehnel waking with a panic attack, the hovering butterfly, and his picture falling down at the funeral, I told her about how Kolton had known about his Poppa being on the tractor without anyone telling him. Lana, my doctor, said, "He's letting you know he's okay and he's still here with you. You will see him again. We are all going to be together again."

I said, "How do you know for sure?"

She told me to read this book, *Forever Ours,* by Janis Amatuzio.

I read the book. Dr. Janis Amatuzio is a forensic pathologist in a coroner's office. She compassionately tells about her spiritual experiences in the morgue with her deceased patients and their families. Then I read Dr. Amatuzio's second book, *Beyond Knowing*. I became obsessed with reading books about the afterlife, grief, the opioid epidemic, addiction, mental illness—books that had anything to do with Jeremy's death. I read books written by mediums and believers in the afterlife such as James VanPraagh, Karen Noe, Kim Russo, Depok Chopra, James Edwards, Linda Jackson, and Teresa Caputo.

Our signs from Jeremy continued, and these books validated that I was not crazy or imagining this. Bob and Jaehnel were getting many signs as well. Some of the other books I read were *When the Bough Breaks*, *Signs from the Afterlife*, *Don't Kiss Them Good-bye*, *Proof of Heaven*, and *The Afterlife of Billy Fingers*. I also read books by parents who had lost children, such as *No One Cares About Crazy People* and *Treasures in Tragedy*.

I also read books about the opioid epidemic, such as *Dopesick and Fentanyl, Inc.* I wanted to understand why so many people are dying and we can't put a stop to it. I wanted to help. I wanted to put some of this pain into purpose. *Dopesick* explains the start of the opioid epidemic as deceptive marketing strategies by pharmaceutical companies. Specifically, encouraging doctors to prescribe opioids even though the companies knew they were highly addictive. When the patients were cut off, they went to the streets for heroin. This created the demand, and drug dealers were only too happy to provide the supply. Then illicit fentanyl and carfentanil were introduced to heroin supplies and sometimes cocaine supplies, causing tens of thousands of deaths across the country. New Jersey joined other states in the lawsuits against roughly two dozen drug industry giants that make or sell opioids. Many feel that this is too little too late for all the people who lost their lives and their loved ones. Some say that government officials share some of the blame because red flags were present years ago when opioid sales were skyrocketing.

(Beth Macy 2018)

Signs

ON THE FIRST OF JULY, we attended a family graduation party. Bob's second cousin Austin had graduated college. It was a cloudy day with breaks of sun and showers. After one of the showers, there was a double rainbow in the sky. Jaehnel said to me that a double rainbow is a sign that someone was here visiting and are on their way back to heaven.

A few days later, Jaehnel was getting Kolty dressed and was looking into his eyes. All of a sudden Kolty, who was not yet three years old, said what Jaehnel was thinking: "My eyes look just like Jeremy's." It's true. He resembles his uncle so much, not only in looks but personality, too. I constantly see glimpses of Jeremy in him.

Another day at the end of July, Jaehnel said Kolty had come into their bedroom in the early morning hours and said he was scared because his sensored nightlight was on and it was daytime. It usually only goes on in the dark. Jaehnel went into his room and sure enough, it was on but it was perfectly light in the room.

Jeremy had given me an urn for my last birthday that had a solar–powered light on top. It had little stars cut out that would shine though when the light inside was powered. When it was kept in the sun long enough it would glow in the dark. He was so excited about it. He thought it was the coolest thing, and it was. After Jeremy's passing, we noticed it would sometimes flash off and on when we were talking about Jeremy. I decided to bring it to Lake George to carry his ashes.

On August 1, our family went to camp on one of the Lake George Islands: Bob and I, Jaehnel, Kevin, and their three boys. Jeremy was looking forward to this trip this summer. He was there, but not in the way we wanted him to be. We had brought a lot of his ashes to spread into the lake. We knew he would approve; it was one of his favorite places. We pulled into our usual launching spot with our boat in tow full of camping gear. While we were getting ready to launch the boat, Jaehnel and I both saw a monarch butterfly fly out of the boat.

Once our boat was completely packed and launched, we went to the ranger station set on an island in the lake. These campsites are only accessible by boat. Once we registered, we headed to our site. It was a beautiful site in a cove on Floating Battery Island. Perfect. Once we got there, Bob and I realized that we were camping right next to the site where Jeremy, Bob, and I camped the year before. I looked out on the lake and remembered Jeremy and his dad out in kayaks together, big smiles on both of their faces. Oh, my heart.

We set up camp, three tents altogether. One was for the two boys, Josiah and Jayden. One was for little Kolty and his parents, and one for Bob and me. The tent that Josiah and Jayden were in had used to be Jeremy's. The next day, Kolton came out of his tent and looked up at the boy's tent. He said, "That used to be my tent but now it's the kids' tent." We all looked at each other in amazement. That's when I knew Jeremy was there with us. He and Kolty had a special connection in life and they still did.

It was a beautiful week. We were able to spend a lot of time swimming, kayaking, fishing, and motorboating. The third day we were there, Jaehnel and I were hiking in the woods. We were talking about whether Jeremy would be happy to have his ashes here. I asked if Jaehnel thought Jeremy was really with us, and something hard fell from a tree right in front of me. We looked around but couldn't see what it was. Jaehnel said, "Do you think that was Jeremy?" and something hard fell right in front of her, too. We searched again and couldn't find anything that would make that sound if it fell. I asked Bob what would be falling from the trees now, and he said, "Nothing."

The last night we were there was when we decided to spread the ashes and have our little memorial service. Jaehnel had brought biodegradable lanterns to float in the lake, so we decided to do it right at dusk. The lake was like glass with the moon shimmering a soft light upon it.

We each spoke before we released a lantern. The boys wrote sweet letters to Uncle Jeremy. I read the poem "Missing You Always."

You never said I'm leaving
You never said goodbye
You were gone before we knew it
And only God knows why.
A million times I needed you
A million times I cried
If love alone could have saved you
You never would have died
In life I loved you dearly

In death I love you still,
In my heart I hold a place
That only you can fill
It broke my heart to lose you
But you didn't go alone,
As part of me went with you
The day God took you home.
(Author Unknown)

The lanterns were beautiful in the moonlight. We watched them scatter across the lake.

Bob stood on the rocks and he was crying. He said, "Jeremy, please give me a sign that you are okay." All of a sudden, all the lanterns started to come together and floated around in a perfect circle. We were all in disbelief. I was still, more or less, trying to rationalize some of the other signs we had received as coincidences, but this to me was absolute proof. For me and the rest of my family, this was the beginning of a spiritual awakening.

Jeremy and Jaehnel circa 1981.

Jeremy 2016.

Christa, Mutti, Renate, Papa, Ruth 1953.

Ruth, Christa, Mutti, Renate, Papa, 1959.

Mutti circa 1941.

Smoke Inhalation Fells Man As House Fire Rages

Blaze Badly Damages Home After Children Are Led To Safety Through Bedroom Window

Oakland — Gerhard Jaehnel was treated for smoke inhalation yesterday morning after his house at 193 Hiawatha Boulevard caught fire, police reported.

Jaehnel was awakened by the smoke, police said, and raced through a burning hall to lead his three children from the 1-story house. They escaped through a bedroom window.

Police said the fire, which seriously damaged the interior of the house apparently began in the propane-gas heating unit.

The fire was investigated yesterday morning by State Policeman Sergeant Harry Card, a propane gas specialist.

The fire was extinguished by a team of 50 firemen led by Chief Vernon Yoeman within an hour, but smoke and water damage had spread throughout the house.

Police said Jaehnel was treated by Doctor John Davy in his local office, and then returned to his home by police. His three daughters, Ruth, 21; Christa, 13; and Ranate, 10, were not injured.

The first-aid squad and five fire trucks were sent to the scene, police reported.

Fire 1963.

Ruth 1964.

Bob, Jeremy, Renate,
Jaehnel, Elissa 1985.

Renate, Jaehnel, Jeremy, Elissa 1978.

Jeremy at 6 months 1978.

Papa's family circa 1937.

Papa and Mutti wedding 1949.

Mutti's family circa 1937.

Jeremy, age 5, in 1982.

Jaehnel's family 2017

Elissa's family 2022.

Support

JEREMY HAD BEEN GONE for two months and I was still barely functioning. I called a friend who had lost her daughter fourteen years ago, and who I remembered attended a support group. She gave me the name and a contact number for the group, the Compassionate Friends. She told me she continues to get signs from her daughter. Her daughter died at 4:44 in the morning. The clock in her room stopped at that time and remains there today. Now she gets an uncanny number of messages that contain the numbers 444.

The closest group to us was about forty minutes away. Bob and I attended our first meeting on the second Thursday in August. It was a large group, maybe thirty people, which was a little intimidating. One of the reasons I wanted to attend was because I wanted to see people who were way ahead of me in their grief. I wanted to see if they could function, if they could smile, if they could experience joy. I felt that I would never be able to do these things again. I felt like I would be an empty shell forever.

The meeting started with everyone introducing themselves and their child that had passed and how and when they died. When it was my turn, I could barely talk. There was another new person that was having difficulty too and I knew this was normal grieving. I knew that every person in that room could barely talk when they came to their first meeting. Everyone was very supportive. I spoke about being so torn about letting people know how and why Jeremy died. They told me not to make the decision yet. They said I would know in time if and who I want to tell. This was very good advice and so very true. It felt good to tell someone, especially among people who would not judge.

August 24 was Kolton's third birthday. Jaehnel and Kevin were still grieving but trying to hold things together for the kids. They weren't up to having a party so we decided to go to Camelbeach, an outdoor water park. The kids had a great time and Kolty especially loved the lazy river and the wave pool.

That night I lay in Jeremy's bed with his ashes for a while and talked to him. I told him how much I missed him and I hoped that somehow, he was with us today for Kolty's birthday.

As soon as I came downstairs, there was a text message on my phone from Jaehnel. She said that when she put Kolty to bed he was talking about what a great birthday he'd had and named everybody who was there. Then he said, "And Jeremy was watching me all day." Jaehnel asked how he knew that and he said, "Maybe Momma or Poppa told me."

A few days later, Jaehnel was putting a picture on her phone screen. It was a picture of Jeremy with his arm around Josiah at Josiah's preschool graduation. He always tried to be there for the kids' celebrations. Suddenly, the graduation cap that Josiah wore fell out of the closet. Jaehnel said she hadn't even remembered where she put the cap!

I was getting so overwhelmed with all these signs. I decided to go to a spiritual fair where you could meet with a psychic or medium for a charge. When I signed up at the fair, I said

I would really like to meet with somebody that had mediumship skills. They mentioned that one of their psychics was particularly good at it, but that she was unable to attend that night. I just let them pick someone else for me. My reading went okay. She told me about a decision I would be making soon that had something to do with finances and that I would make the right decision. Other than that, the reading was rather uneventful.

I decided to make a private appointment with the person they said had great mediumship skills. I got her contact information from their website and made an appointment. On September 5, I met with Susan.

As soon as I sat down with her, she said, "You've lost someone, haven't you?"

I said yes.

She said she could tell by my voice. She said it was someone young. A son. She said, "I think it had something to do with alcohol or drugs." She saw the number five. Jeremy died on June 5. She continued, "He says he is sorry, he thought it was something he could handle and he doesn't want you to feel any guilt whatsoever. He says you were the best parents in the world and there's nothing else you could have done."

It sounded so much like what Jeremy would say. I felt his sobriety coin from AA in my pocket. I thought it would be a better chance of connection if I brought something of his.

She said she saw that Jeremy had recently gone to more of a busy area than he was used to living in and then had come back to where he was used to living, in a more rural area. She continued, telling me that she saw busy fingers. "He had some kind of talent with his hands. Did he play musical instruments?"

"No," I said. "He was very mechanical. Always working on motors, cars, ATVs, motorcycles—for him and his friends."

She said, “If you are working on something, ask for his help and he will help you.” She said “he is very handsome and he is with your father.” My mind started spinning, thinking that maybe this woman had done research on me, because I hadn’t told her anything at all before our meeting. These are things, though, that she could never have found even if there was a place she could have researched. She talked about Jeremy recently getting involved with friends that he didn’t know very well. She told me that he is happy and wants us to be happy. I thought she probably said this part to everyone to bring them comfort. She told me to watch for signs because he would keep sending them. It might be lights flickering or something moving. I was happy to write her a check when I left. My visit was worth every penny. On the way home I talked to Jeremy. I asked, “Was that really you, Jeremy? Please give me some kind of sign so I know.”

That night I woke in the middle of the night and saw a dark male form standing over my bed. I immediately thought Bob had got up to go to the bathroom. I took my arm to feel for him and there he was, still in bed with me. This was my sign. This was Jeremy telling me that it was him coming through the medium. He was watching over us. I stared at the apparition until it was gone. A couple of days later, I got a card in the mail with my check sent back to me from Susan. She said she was so sorry for my loss and was happy that she could provide some comfort. Her sentiment was touching.

Presence

September 14, 2017

IT WAS THE SECOND THURSDAY of September and our second meeting at the Compassionate Friends. It was a speaker meeting and the speaker was a grief counselor. At the end there was a question and answer period. I asked if her clients often report signs from their lost loved ones. She replied, "Oh yes, and they usually start out by saying, 'You're going to think I'm crazy but . . .' Lots of pennies from heaven, etc."

I looked at Bob and said, "That's one sign we have never gotten—pennies or coins."

Wouldn't you know it, in the weeks that followed, Bob, Jaehnel, and I started seeing pennies at the most unusual times. On a line in a store sometimes we would look down and there would be a shiny penny. Jaehnel would wipe off the table and turn around and there would be two pennies on the table. I would find pennies in my pocket or in the middle of a hallway. One day Kolty had one in his sock and his mom asked, "why"? He said because it tickles. Then we started seeing dimes. Sometimes it was a dime and a penny together.

September 23, 2017
When he was about eight years old, Jeremy's favorite song was "Johnny B Good." He made us learn all the words and sing it around the campfire. He just loved that song. On September 23, my niece Taylor got married. It was an outdoor wedding and reception. There was someone in charge of playing music although I wouldn't call him an official DJ. All of a sudden "Johnny B Good" came on. How often do you hear that song played at a wedding reception?

My sister and I were both taking pictures. Both of us had a little light showing up in our pictures. Getting frustrated, we kept deleting our pictures and trying again. Later I remembered reading about "orbs" being a way spirits show their presence in pictures. Jeremy always has a way of showing us his presence at special occasions.

Umbrella Ministries

On September 30, I headed to Ocean City, New Jersey with four other ladies in the Compassionate Friends support group to the Journey of the Heart Retreat for Bereaved Moms. All of our boys died from drugs except for Linda's. Her son died from leukemia but he had suffered from bipolar and addiction as well. I roomed with Debbie. Both our boys were in their thirties when they died. They both died from fentanyl, and her son died about five months before mine.

On the way to the retreat we talked about my visit to the medium. Teresa is the leader of our chapter of Compassionate Friends. She lost her son when he was sixteen, nine years ago. She has been in the Compassionate Friends since and has been to many Umbrella Ministries retreats. She said, "Whatever you do, don't mention going to a medium at the retreat." Some believe you should only go to God to connect with your loved one. There are so many different beliefs. The medium I went to was, in fact, a reverend.

We stayed at the Port-O-Call Hotel right on the beach. The weekend was full of activities that were meant to be healing. There were crafts that included collaging and sharing pictures of our children. There were workshops, a candlelight ceremony, inspirational speakers, music, and walks on the beach. We broke into groups by categories of how our children died. My group was one of several where our children died from drugs. Other categories were suicide, illness, murder, and an accident. Somehow, I thought Jeremy's death could fit into any one of these categories.

In our group we went around the circle and introduced ourselves and our children. It had been three months, but I still couldn't talk when it came to my turn. I just couldn't get the words out. All that came out were tears, and I asked if they could come back to me. Next to me was a mom that was only one month away from her loss and she couldn't talk either. Once we were introduced, we talked not about how our children died but how they lived, which was really very nice. Debbie was in my group. Many in my group had lost their children to fentanyl as well. Many were there from different states.

Whereas the Compassionate Friends is a non-religious group, Umbrella Ministries definitely has a religious feature. It amazed me how some of these moms did not question their faith in God with what they had been through. Most believed that we are not meant to understand why God would take a life so soon, but they seemed to believe that it was meant to be and perhaps our children were spared from something worse that was yet to come. I could not share this belief and questioned my faith. I know many bereaved parents become angry at God, which is understandable. You wonder how any God would make something so terrible happen, although we know that horrible things happen to young people and good people all the time.

One speaker explained it that God took your child away so early because maybe if he didn't, something worse was going to happen. What? What could be worse than losing your life?

But later I thought about this. Many of the moms in my support group meetings had expressed how their children turned into different people. Some of them stole, lied, committed crimes, went to jail, and seemed not to care about anyone or anything except getting that drug. When Jeremy died, he was still loved by everyone who knew him. He never stole from us or from anyone. I never saw him stray from being compassionate and kind. Was this because his experience with heroin, if he used it, was short-lived? We did not have a lengthy period in crisis just preceding his death. If his addiction had grown, would he have turned into a different person? This is something I would not have wanted to see. I can't imagine him being anything but a good person. Sometimes you can find gratitude in the worst of circumstances.

But what about children that have died even younger? People who have had long periods of suffering? Is it possible to find any reasoning, gratitude, or peace in the most horrendous of circumstances? These questions led me on a quest for answers. I read many books on this topic. I learned about lots of different theories. Some authors believe that souls that were here for a shorter time have completed their purpose. That every soul has something to accomplish, learn, or teach to someone else. That they, in fact, probably have had other soul lives before this one and that souls are regenerated. Some of the authors believe that souls choose whether to stay in a spiritual plane or whether to reincarnate on earth again. One book even said that if a person dies of suicide, they don't have the choice. Their soul comes back to earth with the same affliction because they didn't stay for the time they were supposed to stay to fulfill their purpose. Wow. For a time, I even wondered if my son had come back with my mother's soul.

There is also the belief that our life here on earth is predetermined. This is not just a theory of one person, but I have found it to be a common theme of several people who claim to be in touch with the spiritual world. I thought about how Jeremy seemed to know he was going to die before the age of forty. Some of these things are hard for me to believe, but with all the spiritual signs that have taken place, I wouldn't discount anything as impossible.

I began reading different definitions of God. When I was a child, I went to Sunday school and church. I thought of God as someone with human features. After all, we learned that he created Jesus and all of us in his image. But what is He? A spirit, a power? Many people today are moving away from the structure of religions and are striving to find meaning in a less rigid spirituality. I have read a definition of God as "the universe." I have read about the Greeks before Christ who had gods of the moon, the stars, the ocean—many gods. I read about the Pagans before Christ who also had many gods of nature. Buddhism also holds a belief that God is in everything.

Maybe God is the power and energy of all that is Good in the world. I do believe that the things that happen to us are random and happen by chance. Why would some have to suffer so much and some not at all? I do believe in the power of prayer to send love to people, and I do believe that the more people are praying and sending love, the more they can give strength. I know how many people were sincerely praying for us when we lost Jeremy, and I could feel their love giving me strength.

First Birthday in Heaven

For the next several weeks I continued to feel Jeremy's presence and journal every few days. Here are some of my journal entries as Jeremy's first birthday in Heaven approached.

November 11, 2017
Jaehnel told me that Kolty asked her to hold him and rock him in the rocking chair in his bedroom before he went to bed. She said he kept repeating the number 14, 14, 14. Jeremy's birthday was approaching on November 14. The first birthday without him. He would have been forty years old. We didn't know what, if anything, we would do to honor his birthday.

For the next couple of days, we were all finding a phenomenal number of pennies in the most unusual places.

November 13, 2017
Jaehnel heard Kolty crying in his sleep so she went in and said, "Are you okay?"

"I'm just sad," he said.

November 14, 2017
Kolty woke up this morning and said to his mom, "What number is today?"

"What do you mean?" asked Jaehnel.

"The day, what is the number?"

"Well, it's the 14th, November 14."

"Whose birthday is it today?"

"It's Uncle Jeremy's birthday," his mom answered with tears in her eyes.

"Well, then we have to celebrate," said Uncle Jeremy's little buddy.

Jaehnel called me and told me what Kolty had said and we both agreed that we had to have a celebration. We decided that Jeremy was trying tell us through Kolton that he wanted us to be together on his birthday. I ordered pizza, one of Jeremy's favorites, and I baked a cake.

Jaehnel brought a gift for Jeremy. It was a beautiful, hand-carved bench for a garden that we had been working on. It had butterflies carved in it and said "Jeremy, Forever in Our Hearts." It was just beautiful.

It was already a very emotional night, and then Kolty said, "When is Jeremy going to get here?" He thought he was finally going to see him after five months and was so excited.

Jaehnel said, "Oh, honey, remember what we said, that we won't actually be able to see him, but we feel him in our hearts and we can talk to him and think of him."

Kolty got so teary-eyed. My already broken heart splintered some more. Later on, he blew out the candles for his Uncle Jeremy. It must be so hard for little ones to understand. It's hard for me to understand.

First Christmas in Heaven

December 23, 2017
I was wrapping presents and crying. It was a difficult Christmas with being the first one with Jeremy gone. My phone was lying on the bed and I saw a message on my phone, "I'm Sorry," I picked it up and was in shock. I tried to fiddle with my phone to determine how it could have appeared like that but there was no way that my phone could have done this on its own. Jeremy had sent me a message, for sure.

There was also an "okay" message with an okay sign emoji, but I didn't put it there. When I clicked on it, it said "not deliverable." I tried again and it wouldn't send. Jaehnel called me and asked if I sent her a message that said "okay." She said she was just waiting to meet her ex-husband to pick up Josiah and she was sitting there talking to Jeremy and wishing she knew if he was okay and she got the message that said "okay" with the okay sign from my phone. I thought, how strange, because my phone said I didn't send it and it was undeliverable. It had to be Jeremy sending her a message using my phone to do it.

December 22, 2017
Jaehnel told me that Kevin heard wood chopping outside at night. He went outside and started to walk toward it but it got quieter. When he started walking back to the house it got louder.

December 27, 2017
Jaehnel was in line at Walmart. She has a button with a picture of Jeremy that she always wears on her purse. There was a young girl in a wheelchair behind her signaling to the button on Jaehnel's purse. Her mom said, "She wants to know who that it is and how old."

Jaehnel said, "My brother, he's thirty-nine."

Her mom said, "She lost an older brother, too. She knew that was your brother and you lost him, too."

The Lives They Loved

AS TIME WENT ON, I felt a little less broken, which I attribute mostly to my connection to Jeremy, all the signs we received, and feeling that, at least in some way, he was still here with us.

Sometime in December, my friend sent me a link to *The New York Times Magazine*. As part of the magazine's annual "The Lives They Lived" issue, they invited readers to contribute a photograph and a story of someone close to them who died this year, and called it "The Lives They Loved." I decided to enter. The first couple of days into January, a friend messaged me and had read my story. I hadn't even known at the time that mine was one of the ones selected to be published. It was limited to four hundred words, so I had to keep cutting it. I included what I had written in his eulogy, but added the following:

Jeremy had bipolar disorder. It was diagnosed when he was seventeen—we thought we had already lost the son we knew, but after starting medication, he gradually came back to us. The medication stabilized him but came with unpleasant side effects that caused Jeremy to sometimes try to lower or go off it. Each time led to a disaster that he somehow survived, until the last time.

Jeremy thought he had found his own self-medication in cocaine. It gave him the energy that his illness and lithium took away. He could work twelve hours a day and still have energy. He thought he had found the answer to being the person he wanted to be. One day, a drug dealer decided to cut Jeremy's drug with fentanyl to make more money. Jeremy died and left all his family heartbroken forever. The drug dealer didn't care. Let Jeremy's story teach us about living. At first, we felt that letting people know would be a breach of Jeremy's privacy, but then we realized that this kind soul who wanted to befriend every elderly person and small child and bring home every stray animal he came across would want us to tell his story and help save lives. Remember Jeremy. We love and miss him forever and always.

The Signs Continue

January 5, 2018
Kolty said to his mom, "When I was your size, you and I used to ride on Big Wheels. You would ride behind me and we would spin out." This was true. Jeremy was talking through his nephew again. Amazing. There was no way Kolty knew anything about this. It was thirty-five years before he was born! Jaehnel said, "How do you know that?" He said, "I don't know, I just know."

January 28, 2018
Kolty said to his mom, "Remember when we were babies together?" I started to wonder if Kolton would grow up to be someone with a special spiritual ability.

February 9, 2018
In between these times, we had also continued to find shiny pennies and dimes in the most peculiar places. Today was Josiah's birthday, and Jaehnel asked Jeremy for a sign that he was there for Josiah's birthday. We had just finished dinner and cake and she wiped off the table. She turned around after, knowing she had just cleaned off the table, and held up a penny. He never disappoints!

February 10, 2018
I was talking to Jeremy, thanking him for leaving a sign that he was there for Josiah's birthday. I told him to keep the signs coming because they mean so much to me. All of a sudden, the doorbell cover on the wall fell to the floor. I have been living in this house for thirty-four years and that has never happened before.

February 13, 2018
Like so many days, I had tears thinking about Jeremy. Lucky, the cat, wanted to go out so I opened the door. There was a shiny dime on the step. I knew it wasn't there before and no one had come in and out. These coins always show up when I'm thinking about him and talking to him. We find them in our pockets, on the floor, outside— everywhere and anywhere.

The Grief Recovery Program

IT HAD BEEN EIGHT MONTHS and I was still so heavy in my grief. I was trying to function the best I could. I was retired from my full time social work job but was still working part-time doing workshops in schools through CAP (Child Assault Prevention Program). We do empowering programs, for pre-K through teens, about bullying, stranger danger, and sexual assault. Being distracted with something else that required a lot of concentration helped me. However, holding it together for a length of time was exhausting. Grief is exhausting. Sometimes I would just burst into tears on the way home or when I got home. It was a release of trying so hard to hold it together that long.

When I visited my doctor again, I fell apart in her office. She insisted that even though I was going to a support group, I needed professional grief counseling. She gave me a card that was left in her office for someone right in the same town as me. I looked at the name: Joan Cehak, Grief Recovery. I knew that name. Bob and Jeremy had done quite a bit of work for Joan.

I called Joan and told her I was interested in grief therapy and told her I hadn't realized she was a therapist. She immediately asked who it was that I lost. When I told her it was Jeremy, she got very upset. I believe she was very fond of Jeremy, and vice-versa.

She explained that she was not, in fact, a therapist, but had taken a weekend certification course from the Grief Recovery Institute when she was grieving terribly for her husband who she lost eleven years prior. Her husband was in his eighties, but his passing was unexpected. She'd had a very difficult time with grief for quite a few years. She was more than willing to do the program with me, so we made plans for our first appointment. She told me to get the book, *The Grief Recovery Handbook*.

When I got the book, I read through the whole thing, even though it is designed to complete in steps with a partner. It was described as an action program for moving beyond death, divorce, and other losses. On the back of the book it said, "*The Grief Recovery Handbook* offers grievers the specific actions needed to complete the grieving process and accept loss." I was immediately skeptical. When it comes to losing a son or daughter, I don't really think the grieving process is ever complete and the loss is ever really accepted.

The program involved three major homework assignments. The first one was completing a loss history graph—a graph of all the losses in your life, and then identifying your greatest loss. You then complete a relationship graph with the person that was your greatest loss. All the positive experiences were graphed above a median line across the page and all the negative experiences below the line. Every negative experience on my chart had to do with Jeremy's illness. We then converted the relationship graph to recovery components. The recovery components fell into three categories: Amends, Forgiveness, and Significant Emotional Statements. The final homework assignment was writing a Grief Recovery Completion Letter to your lost loved one. I had difficulty with this because this process seemed more for someone who had an incomplete relationship with their loved one and had unresolved relationship issues. This wasn't the case for Jeremy and me. We always had a great relationship. He often told me how much he appreciated everything I did for him and he didn't know where he'd be without me. We were close. There was a strong bond and great love between us. However, I sat down and did my best with the letter:

Dear Jeremy,

In reviewing our relationship, I need to tell you that you have given me both the happiest and saddest days of my life. Dad and I were so happy when we found out you were coming and we wanted you so much. The day you were born was pure bliss. I remember fearing that I loved you so much that I may not have been able to love a second baby as much. Of course, I realized how untrue that was when your sister was born. You quickly built a compassionate best-friend relationship with her that was loving and protective. I know that relationship continues until this day and will forever.

You always had a remarkable love of life and people and have such a kind soul. I'll never forget one day when I was substitute teaching at Blairstown and I was in the teachers' lounge. One of your old teachers was there and he told me you were the nicest kid he ever met. That was quite a compliment coming from a teacher of thirty-five years.

I am so sorry that you inherited a horribly difficult disease that made the latter part of your life such a struggle. As your mom, I feel I should have been able to save you and protect you. I always wonder if there was something I could have done that would have changed the course of things. Were our messages against drugs not strong enough to scare you away from them? Did I try hard enough to talk you into staying home that weekend? I had a feeling something wasn't right with you and something bad was going to happen. Your dad said you were an adult and I had to let you go and I know that's true. We had no control over your choices. You can only do the best you can with what you know at the time, so I am trying to say goodbye to the guilt.

I forgive you for the choices you made because I can't be angry at you for something that was out of your control.

This is the point I'm supposed to say good-bye but I can't say good-bye to you. I will say good-bye to your physical presence on earth but I know our relationship continues even though it is in a different way. My love for you still grows. You are one of a kind and I try to remember how lucky we are every day to have you as a son. You made a difference in this world when you were here and we know that you will continue to lead us in making a difference in your name. Please keep sending us signs to let us know you are near. They are always a comfort. We all love and miss you so much. Until we meet again.

Love, Mom

The best part of working this program with Joan was just that, working the program with Joan. We became very close and I was so comfortable knowing that she shared my spiritual beliefs and that we had read many similar books and had tried similar methods, such as meditation. We became friends, and it was such a comfort knowing that she knew Jeremy. What a coincidence that I had been given her card. Or, are there any coincidences when it comes to matters like this?

At our last session of grief work, Joan said when I left, "When you're talking to Jeremy thank him for fixing my roof. It's still good." On the way home I told Jeremy just that and told him I would love another sign. I headed to the bus stop to pick up the boys. While I was waiting, I found a dime folded in the material around the stick shift in the car.

Parents Helping Parents

April 11, 2018

I saw an advertisement online for a new support group at The Center for Prevention & Counseling. It was called Parents Helping Parents and was for parents who had lost their children to drugs or alcohol. I was very familiar with the Center. When I did social work for the Department of Child Protection and Permanency (DCPP), we worked with them a lot. They had many valuable programs that we could refer our clients to.

I asked for Rachel as it said to do in the ad. When I talked to her, I asked, "Is this the Rachel that worked for St. Clare's?" It turned out that this Rachel was one and the same. When I worked for DCPP, she wasn't working for the Center but for St. Clare's Hospital in mental health and we had had several mutual clients. Rachel and I had also crossed paths after that. When Jeremy was twenty-six and was in AA, her ex-husband was his sponsor. They were so fond of one another. Brian was like a big brother to him. Jeremy still had Brian's six-month pin that he gave him when Jeremy reached six months sober. Jeremy had spent quite a bit of time at Rachel and Brian's home. Rachel and I both cried. We both believed Jeremy brought us together again.

Lucky Goes Home

June 2, 2018

Our cat, Lucky, was brought home by Jeremy about eleven years ago. She is an indoor and outdoor cat. One morning, she cried by the door to go out so I opened the door and out she went. Seconds later she slammed against our sliding glass door and a large cat slammed into the door after her. We immediately got up to look at what the heck was going on. A bobcat was chasing Lucky on our deck. It grabbed her by the neck and killed her. Bob went outside and the bobcat was waiting on the sidelines to eat his prey. Bob shot his shotgun to scare him away.

We were shocked. We knew our area was considered somewhat of a sanctuary for bobcats. Some were brought here in the '80s from Maine because they were considered endangered species. I never thought they would come that close to the house. I reported the event to Fish and Wildlife and they kept saying what unusual behavior that was for a bobcat.

Later, I was on the phone with my friend Debbie and I told her about the bobcat. Debbie and I belong to the same support group and her son died in similar circumstances as

Jeremy. Debbie said, "Well, maybe Jeremy wanted his cat to be with him."

I saw Debbie a couple of days later at the next support group meeting and she said, "I have to tell you something. The day after I talked to you, my cat that was Ray's cat, that he brought home, was playing with a frog that ended up being venomous. I noticed that she was sick, lethargic, and her mouth was foaming. I brought her to the vet but she passed away. I think Ray was jealous that Jeremy had his cat and Ray wanted his!" Debbie and I had decided long ago that our boys were together "up there" and brought us together "down here."

Brain and Behavior Research

FOUR DAYS AFTER JEREMY DIED, I was talking to my stepmother on the phone. I think my family and friends got used to me crying through phone conversations. My stepmother had remarried after my father died. She had been married to my father for twenty years and to her next husband for thirteen years before he passed on as well. She and her husband had a charitable fund. Her husband had left her in charge of it and requested that she keep up with certain charities that were important to him, but left her the option of making choices of her own for charitable donations. She explained that she would love to do something in Jeremy's name, maybe to help others. She wanted the decision to be up to me, Bob, and Jaehnel.

I was touched by this offer and wanted to make a careful decision. I wanted to make sure the donation was meaningful. I started researching by calling the National Association for Mental Illness. I had been a member and attended some of their classes and support groups. I explained my situation and asked if they had any suggestions about where there was the greatest need. The woman I spoke with asked me to think about where I wanted to make the most difference. I thought about it and said, "Well, my dream would be for there to be a cure for bipolar and other biological mental illnesses." With that, she suggested I might want to look into the Brain and Behavior Research Foundation. They are devoted to finding better treatments and cures. I thanked her and thought that it was so nice of her to want to make sure our charitable contribution went to what would mean the most. I know NAMI is a wonderful organization and they do a lot for mental illness. She could have easily talked me into contributing to one of their programs.

I looked into the Brain and Behavior Research Foundation. They are an organization that funds doctors and researchers pursuing new, innovative research investigations. One hundred percent of their donations go to research because they have a family foundation that funds all their administrative costs. You could fund research in $30,000 grants. Each investigator had to submit their idea and submit the details of their research, how it would be conducted, and what results they hoped to achieve. I spoke to the woman in charge of fundraising. Her name was, very appropriately, Faith. She was kind and compassionate while listening to my story. I told her we would like to sponsor research on bipolar. She had a way of weeding out all the research that had to do with bipolar and sent me about a dozen to read over. We decided to keep it in the tri-state area, in case I ever wanted to meet the researcher in person or visit their laboratory.

Reading over each scientist's research ideas was overwhelming. Much of it was written in very scientific language. I finally picked one that was about bipolar disorder and gene expression through the National Institute of Mental Health. I spoke to the doctor that was leading this research once in person and also through e-mail. He told me that he does see a future possibility in gene editing to cure bipolar disorder but that probably neither of us would see that day. I didn't expect to see the day but it was comforting that there was some promise for future generations. The individual scientist who we had sponsored had to leave the National Institute for Mental Health for a full-time job offer. However, his group of researchers was continuing the work at the National Institute for Mental Health.

We were able to choose a second investigator as well, who was working on bipolar disorder and its connection to addiction.

This whole experience with the Brain and Behavior Research Foundation was enlightening for me. I always thought that there was not enough being done for mental illness or substance use disorder but this organization and the brilliant, caring people in it gave me a whole new sense of hope.

There is so much research going on in this organization, not just for bipolar but any disease of the brain, which includes addiction, ADHD, anxiety, autism, borderline personality disorder, depression, eating disorders, OCD, Parkinson's, panic disorder, psychosis, PTSD, schizophrenia, suicide, and others. They also have many studies that encompass two or more disorders together.

I was invited to a dinner at the Metropolitan Club in New York hosted by the Brain and Behavior Research Foundation. I was allowed to bring two guests, so I brought my Jaehnel and one of my best friends, Antonette. I met Faith in person. She had planned the seating arrangements and told me she thought I would be happy with the people at my table. Feeling initially a little intimidated, being surrounded by brilliant doctors, scientists, and researchers, I soon realized there was no reason to be. Faith had very strategically placed the right people at our table.

There were three doctors that did research on bipolar disorder, one that was working on trying to make medication-assisted treatment more available to the addicted, and a gentleman who had lost his son in a skateboarding accident when he was thirteen. We immediately felt comfortable with our company. The speakers were so interesting, talking about their dedication to addiction, depression, and other mental illnesses. I realized I should have known that only a compassionate, kind person would dedicate their life and skills to improving the lives of the mentally ill. I left that dinner with newfound hope.

The Brain and Behavior Research Foundation has become one of my favorite charitable organizations. They do so much to improve the lives of the mentally ill, which includes substance use disorder. I often receive updates of progress from them. They have recently finished a study that reveals how bipolar disorder emerges in high-risk youth. A child of a parent with bipolar has a 24.5 percent risk that they will develop bipolar illness. This study was expected to help doctors to diagnose bipolar disorder in young people. The illness typically unfolds in a progressive sequence between the ages of twelve and thirty. Symptoms are not usually obvious in the younger ages of this spectrum and can overlap with several other disorders, as well as just be symptoms of adolescence.

One of the study's findings is that childhood sleep and anxiety disorders are important predictors of emerging bipolar disorder. I remember that when Jeremy was about eight years old, he would have trouble getting to sleep. He would keep getting up, and very frustrated, would say, "I can't sleeeep! Can I please have some Benadryl?" I never gave him Benadryl to sleep but he learned that it made him tired when he took it sometimes for allergies. Then there was his anxiety about going to school.

A diagnosis usual comes with an episode of mania, hypomania, and/or a first episode of psychosis, which usually follows a period of major depression. In this study, no child met diagnostic criteria for a bipolar diagnosis before the age of twelve. Jeremy had that period of depression and anxiety at the age of fourteen. Jeremy's youth fits the overall model of emerging bipolar disorder perfectly. There were the childhood symptoms not specific to bipolar, such as sleep problems and anxiety symptoms to minor mood disorders, then adolescent major depressive disorder, and finally a full-blown bipolar disorder in the transition to adulthood. This is an important topic to study because early treatment in bipolar disorder and other brain and behavior disorders generates better outcomes for patients. These are valuable facts for us all to be aware of.

(Ann Duffy M.D. 2019)

That night after the Brain and Behavior dinner, we took the ferry across the river to New Jersey and stayed at a hotel on the New Jersey side. I slept in the bed next to the window with the drapes open. It was a full moon and I wanted to look at it. There was one lonely, bright star by the moon. Actually, I think it might have been Venus. I talked to Jeremy silently and said good night to him through that star, hoping it was a window to heaven.

The next day we came home and Jaehnel said to Kolton, "I missed you."

He said, "I missed you, too. I was calling, 'Mommy, Mommy.'"

Jaehnel said, "I blew you a kiss before I went to bed. Did you get it?"

He said, "Yes, and Jeremy got the kiss you blew to the stars."

One Year

June 5, 2018

It was one year since Jeremy left us. I had not one but three signs. I saw a cardinal outside, found a penny, and the towel had once again fallen from the towel rack. Somehow, I thought that one year would be some sort of milestone; that I would be better. I had been through the first birthday, Thanksgiving, Christmas, New Year's, Mother's Day, and his Angel Day (Day of Death). This is a fallacy. I wasn't better.

Many moms in my support group said, in some ways, the second year is even harder. You have forced yourself out from under the covers, gone to work, forced smiles, but it was all in a state of numbness you created to protect yourself, to function. I had made it through the first year but I was still so heavy in my grief.

June 8, 2018

Rachel, who runs our support group, Parents Helping Parents, asked if I would speak at the annual Overdose Awareness Day Candlelight Vigil. They usually have a parent as one of the speakers. I immediately accepted. I truly felt that I was being guided by Jeremy. I no longer worried that he would be upset about my openness and honesty surrounding his death. I felt that he was proud of me; that we were working together to help people, to increase awareness, and to make a difference.

June 10, 2018
I had recently gotten involved with the CARE coalition. (Community Addiction Response Education) whose mission was to raise awareness about the presence, dangers and negative impact of substance use in our communities. Today we were creating a video public service announcement. Parents who lost their children would hold up handmade signs and were to be filmed at various town landmarks.

Jaehnel, Kolton, and I met with the Blairstown CARE Coalition in town. We all introduced each other. Kolton is usually very shy meeting people but he was so different today. As each person said their name, he shook their hand and said, "Hello, Lena. Hello, Eric. Hello, Dave. Hello, Kevin. Hello, Mr. Bob." He repeated each name. This is something he wouldn't normally do. He sounded just like someone I knew when he would meet people. Yes, he sounded just like his Uncle Jeremy. That's when I knew Jeremy was there with us.

We wrote our messages on a little chalkboard with chalk. I wrote, "My son was a beautiful person." Jaehnel wrote, "My brother, my best friend." We chose the town park for the first filming location. I could not hold back tears during the filming and neither could the crew. I saw the grown men had tears in their eyes.

Later that afternoon, we attended a butterfly release. I had purchased a butterfly in Jeremy's name and so did my friend, Antonette. It was a wet day so they couldn't let all the butterflies go. The next day, Antonette, Kolton, and I went to the hospice with a beautiful view of the mountain where they released the rest of the butterflies. Butterflies are a symbol of new life in a different form. When I got home that day, the bath towel had fallen of the bath rack onto the floor.

June 11, 2018
One year since Jeremy's funeral day. Kolton talked about Jeremy all day. He talked about when Jeremy sold his truck and bought a car. Kolton said, "Jeremy said it was an old man's truck." Kolton also said, "Jeremy used to play with me upstairs all the time."

July 3, 2018
For the first Christmas after we lost Jeremy, I picked out and ordered my own gift. As I mentioned earlier, the last card that Jeremy had given me was on Mother's Day, 2017. On the card he wrote, "I love you so much. You mean so much to me. Love, Jeremy." I had found a website that made jewelry inscribed with a person's handwriting. I took a picture of the inscription on the card and ordered a bracelet. I didn't open it until Christmas morning and it was perfect. There it was, that beautiful message in Jeremy's handwriting.

My niece Erin had organized a family reunion along Lake Champlain in Vermont this year from July 1 to July 8. We had rented an RV and planned to go from July 1 to July 5. Family was coming and going throughout the whole week. It was a beautiful week, in the mid-90s, which is a heat wave for Vermont. It was great to be with family. Jaehnel, Kevin, and the boys came up with us and stayed in the RV with us. It was hard to stay out of the lake because it was so hot, so we did a lot of swimming. On July 3, the third day we were there, Kolton and I were heading into the lake for a swim and suddenly Kolton said, "Momma! Your bracelet, you have to take it off so it doesn't get ruined." I did, but he surprised me! I didn't even think he knew how or why that bracelet was so special to me. What three-year-old is aware of and worried about jewelry getting ruined in the water? Then I realized, it's a family reunion, of course Jeremy is here! When it was time to take the family picture of everyone, I ran to the RV to get Jeremy's picture and held it in the photo.

July 5, 2018
We returned home from the beautiful family reunion. I walked into our bedroom and there was a shiny penny on the floor with a feather next to it. I know it wasn't there when we left. It was clearly visible and I would have picked it up. I started unpacking and a shiny dime fell out of the suitcase.

July 17, 2018
Bob and I decided to rent a house with a friend down at the Brigantine shore in New Jersey. We rented it from July 14 to July 21. Jaehnel and the boys came from July 17 to July 20. I was so happy they were coming. We were a one-block walk from the beach and a one-block walk to the bay. We brought our little motorboat, the kayaks, and the bicycles. Before Jaehnel's family arrived, I walked down the hallway to our bathroom. While I was walking back, I saw a shiny penny, smack in the middle of the hallway. It was clearly visible, and I knew it wasn't there before. No one else had walked down the hallway. Jaehnel and her boys would be arriving any minute, but I think Jeremy had already arrived.

August 4, 2018
My whole family participated in the Changing the Face of Addiction Walk. The walk has been an annual event for the past four years. It was started by two ladies in my support group, Parents Helping Parents. They both lost their boys and started the walk in their names. My team, Team Jeremy, was one of the top fund-raising teams. All the money raised went

to the Center for Prevention & Counseling for people who could not afford treatment.

It was an emotional but uplifting day. There were ten of us there walking for Team Jeremy. Buttons and T-shirts were provided and we also made some of our own buttons. They only had adult T-shirts, so Jaehnel made "Team Jeremy" shirts for my grandsons. While we walked, a hovering butterfly flew around our group and stayed with us almost all the way through the walk.

We took some pictures and there is one picture of Kolty holding his Jeremy button and looking up so seriously to the sky. That night when he was going to bed, he asked his mom to open the blinds so he could look into the stars. He reached his arms out toward the window and said, "I need to see Jeremy's face, his real face." I do too, buddy; I do, too.

August 7, 2018

We had garage door installers at our house today by a father and son team. At one point, the father asked Bob how many children he had. Bob said he had a daughter and son but his son had recently passed away. Later in the day, he asked Bob, "Do you mind me asking you how your son died?" Bob told him. He started to cry and said, "I don't know how I knew but I just knew you were going to say that. Would you do me a favor and talk to my son? He was in the emergency room two weeks ago and almost died from a fentanyl overdose. They brought him back with Narcan after several tries."

Bob did talk to him, and told him how lucky he was and about our son not being so lucky. He said the experience truly scared him and he never planned on trying it again. He thought he was taking heroin, not fentanyl. He had been doing it on and off on weekends but this scared him enough to stop. He felt that he could. I hope he's right. I do believe that certain people finding each other is meant to be and I think this was one of those circumstances.

August 9, 2018
My sister-in-law, two nieces, and my nephew came to visit us for a few days. They were on their way home from a trip cross-country. One morning we looked out the window towards Jeremy's garden and the sun was shining right through a perfectly circular spider web between the branches in a tree in the garden. Jeremy loved family visits and get-togethers. He was showing us that he was here with us.

August 23, 2018
It was the day before Kolton's fourth birthday. We were outside and Kolton wanted to go into Jeremy's garden. He reminded us again about all the things that Jeremy worked on in the yard: the fence, the grass, the garden, the butterfly house.

August 24, 2018
We sang "Happy Birthday" to Kolton. He blew out the candles. The lights blinked on and off. I knew Jeremy would let us know he was here for Kolton's birthday.

August 26, 2018
We were celebrating my grandson Jayden's eleventh birthday. We sang, he blew out the candles, and again there was a browning out of the lights. Jeremy always tries to let us know he is here for special occasions.

National Overdose Awareness Vigil

THE LAST DAY of August was the National Overdose Awareness Day event. All over the country, communities were joining together to remember our lost loved ones and spread awareness of this horrible epidemic. As I said earlier, I was asked to speak. I was nervous to speak in front of so many people about such an emotional topic. I was scheduled to go right after the Sussex County Prosecutor and before Father Grider, who would add the names of those lost at the end of his speech. I apologize if this is a repetitive part of my story, but this is my story. I tell it over and over and I will forever.

My name is Renate. I'm here to tell you a little bit about my son Jeremy. He was born on November 14, 1977. We hoped and wished for him and he was a beautiful answer to our prayers. We wanted and loved him so much. When his sister was born thirteen months later, he quickly became her best friend and protector. I know that relationship continues to this day and will forever. From a toddler, Jeremy had such remarkable love of life and people.

My son Jeremy's bipolar disorder surfaced when he was seventeen. So did his first drug use. We thought we already lost the son we knew, but with medication he slowly came back to us and he experienced a long period of stability and sobriety. He was able to successfully finish high school and go away to complete technical school. Unfortunately, the most effective medicine for bipolar does not come without side effects. This caused Jeremy to sometimes try to lower or go off his medicine.

Another bipolar episode in his mid-twenties brought on a second wave of substance use. This time the reintroduction of medicine, intensive outpatient treatment, and a year of twelve-step meetings brought the longest period of stability yet. For the next thirteen years Jeremy talked about the evils of drugs and how he would never do them again, feeling guilty that he may have worsened his bipolar disorder. We truly thought he had won the battle. We were, of course, shocked when we learned on June 5, 2017, he had lost his battle with the co-occurring disorders of bipolar and addiction. I will never forget the pain of receiving the call from the coroner's office. I will never forget it because I carry that pain with me every day and will forever. Several weeks later the toxicology report revealed that he had stopped taking his lithium and died from fentanyl. Since fentanyl has infiltrated our communities, deaths have tripled. Only two milligrams is a fatal dose. Very few people decide to try these drugs with the knowledge of its contents.

Currently, more often than not, drugs sold as heroin are either partially or entirely fentanyl and this is also often found to be true of drugs sold as cocaine. Fentanyl has become a weapon of mass destruction and as long as there is a demand for it along with other drugs and money to be made, it will continue. Over 70,000 overdose deaths were reported in 2018 and the majority contained fentanyl. I know that Congress, the DEA and law enforcement are taking steps to reduce drug trafficking and we have to hope and pray that they continue to be successful. What can we do at this end to reduce the demand for drugs? We need to teach our youth and teach them well. We need to give them the message, "Not Even Once." It may have been Jeremy's first time or his fiftieth time, we didn't know, no one knew. He still would have died. Remember, nowadays, you don't know what's in that drug.

I, myself, cannot talk about addiction without talking about mental illness and suicide, because, you see, in my family they intersect and all three have had a profound impact. Overdose and suicide are both usually an escape from physical or psychic pain. Sometimes we don't even know if an overdose was accidental or intentional.

For Jeremy his substance use was a symptom of his bipolar disorder. Of course, not everyone has a dual diagnosis. Substance use disorder can quickly become an illness in itself, whether started to relieve pain or through experimentation. Brain diseases such as bipolar disorder, depression and addiction all hijack the brain into distorted thinking. We need to treat these like the diseases they are.

We need comprehensive and effective treatment programs and insurance that covers realistic time periods for recovery. We need to make mental health a priority and encourage our youth to share if they are experiencing problems.

So please remember and spread the message, "Not Even Once." Our children are dying. The numbers increase every day. It's too late for Jeremy, but I hope others can be saved.

In the middle of my speech, the church bells one block away tolled. I wondered why they were ringing. It was about 7:50 P.M. It was not a certain hour like 6:00 P.M. or 12:00 P.M. It added something beautiful to my speech. Maybe it was Jeremy and the other lost children of the parents that were before me, listening to me.

At the end of my speech, the audience clapped and clapped and clapped. It seemed like they would never stop. They finally did and I went down into the crowd to join them. Parents came to hug me with tears in their eyes. The pastor and police officers also hugged me. We are all on the same side and we are all in this together. After my speech, Father Grider gave his speech and then the reading of all the names: our children lost. The names went on and on and on. This was only a list of those known to be lost in our community. There are so many more.

The choir sang after the speeches. Their voices were beautiful as day turned into dusk. When they were finished and filing out, several came out of line to come over and hug me. I was overwhelmed by it all but I was happy with my speech. I could tell it made an impact, which I wanted it to do.

The next day a reporter from the local paper called me and talked to me. There would be an article in the paper about the event the next day. I got the paper and read the article. I was quoted—as a mom whose son's bipolar disorder eventually lead him to a fentanyl overdose—as saying, "At first I wasn't sure if telling my son's story would be a breach of his privacy, but he was a good person and I know he would want his story to help save others."

Butterfly, Pennies, and Lights

September 3, 2018

IT WAS MONDAY, Labor Day. Jaehnel, Kevin, the kids, Bob, and I all had it off of work and school. It was a very hot day. We decided to go to Belvidere Pool for the last day of summer vacation. We walked in with our bags, towels, chairs, looking for a nice spot, not too sunny but not too shady. Suddenly, Bob looked down and in the blades of grass shines a bright penny that he picks up. A little later, a black butterfly appeared and hovered around us the rest of the day, whether we were in the water or on the grass.

September 11, 2018

Bob was playing with Kolton. They were pretending they were hunting. Kolton said, "Remember, years ago, we would hunt together and bring snacks?" Bob looked at him in amazement. Yes, Jeremy used to hunt with his dad when he was little and he always wanted to bring a lot of snacks. His dad would joke that Jeremy would scare all the deer away crunching away on the snacks. Then, when the snacks were gone, Jeremy was ready to go home. I did read in one book that spirits can sometimes talk through certain individuals that have the gift of clairaudience. Our little Kolton must have this gift.

September 15, 2018
Bob and I went to dinner with our friends Andy and Pam to the Jefferson House right on Lake Hopatcong. Although the music was a little loud, we were lucky enough to get a table right next to the water so we could watch the sunset. We hadn't seen Andy and Pam in a while so we started talking a lot about our loss and how we were doing. I started talking about all the things that I've gotten involved in which seem to help a bit and of course, I started telling them about all the signs we have received. Suddenly, Bob said, "Look under your chair." I looked and there was a shiny penny. It was so bright and so noticeable. We all said it wasn't there before; we would have noticed it. None of us had taken out our wallets or anything yet. I love you, too, Jeremy.

September 28, 2018
It was evening and I was once again at the funeral home where Jeremy's visitation took place. A good friend, Susan, had passed away five days previously. She died from a blood clot a week after having knee replacement surgery. Not only was Susan a good friend, but her husband was a good friend of Bob's, their son a good friend of Jeremy's, and their daughter a good friend of Jaehnel's. They had all been at this same funeral home one year and three months ago for Jeremy. Jeremy had spent quite a bit of time at their home. When I was getting ready for the funeral, I was feeling very emotional. I can feel the hurt of every loss so much more since the loss of Jeremy. The lights in the bathroom blinked on and off. I knew he was with me and was feeling it too.

At the funeral home, Susan's husband Glen said, "You know, I'm kind of in a fog and forgetting everyone's name, but as each one approaches, Susan seems to be reminding me of their name, and so far, I've gotten everyone right." I believe it, Glen.

As we approached Chris, Susan's son and Jeremy's friend, he said, "You know, I feel Jeremy with me." I believe you, Chris.

At their home the next day, there was a celebration of spirit for Susan at her family's home. We were in the dining room where all the food was and the lights flickered. Glen said, "Did that air conditioner go on again? Sometimes the lights act up when it's on." Bob and I just looked at each other. We knew it wasn't the air conditioner.

Just then, Glen told a little story about how Susan had been on his case to cut down a tree in the front yard because it was dead and she was afraid it was going to fall down and hurt someone. This morning a huge branch fell off the tree that Susan has been asking him to cut down. I told Glen, "Oh, you will see signs. Watch out for them and be open to them."

October 2, 2018

I signed up for a four-week Grief Lecture Series presented by our local Hospice Program. Bob went to the first couple of classes with me. The classes were held at one of our local hospitals. We had to walk through the cafeteria to get to the conference room where the class was being held. We also had to walk back though the cafeteria to go to the bathrooms during breaks. The cafeteria tables were empty since it was not a lunch or dinner hour. When the first class was over, Bob and I walked through the cafeteria toward the exit. There at the end of one of the cafeteria tables sat a bright, shiny penny. Bob and I both looked at it and Bob picked it up. Now, we had walked past that table several times and would have noticed if the penny was there. I think Jeremy was glad that we were trying to do everything we could to get better.

Bob came to one more class with the Grief Lecture Series and I continued going to three more. There were two things I took away from those classes that helped me the most. The instructor talked about how you can't blame yourself or someone else for something that they did not know. We do the best we can with what we know at the time and that's all we can expect. As they say, hindsight is 20/20. It's strange, it's not that I didn't know that or think about it before, but just hearing someone else say it made me feel better. I think it helped me stop blaming myself, my husband, Jeremy, and his friends. Another thing she said was, "You can't control someone else's life or their decisions if they're an adult." This is so true, and also helped me with my guilt feelings.

October 7, 2018
I participated in the 5K Out of the Darkness Walk for Suicide Prevention. There are different colored beads that signify who you lost to suicide and then there are blue beads that signify that you are walking because you support the cause. I wore blue beads, gold beads, and white beads. Gold beads are for loss of a parent and white beads are for loss of a child. I know Jeremy's cause of death was not officially suicide, but to me, it was kind of a suicide in slow motion.

October 12, 2018
My husband Bob is mostly retired but still does small jobs for people, especially people that he knows well. On this day Bob was doing a job for Pat Tanis. Her family owns the local A-Tech where we usually bring our cars if they need repair and are no longer under warranty. Bob had done quite a bit of work for the Tanises before with Jeremy at his side. Pat Tanis told Bob she loved him and Jeremy as a team, and she feels Jeremy brought them together. She'll never forget the day that Jeremy came in to A-Tech and she was telling him

about work that she needed done on her house, and he said, "My Dad and I could do the work."

Two days later Bob finished the work at the Tanises home, but this time without Jeremy by his side. Ms. Tanis hugged him and said, "You're the best." I think Jeremy was there by his side after all.

October 13, 2018
Kolton's dad, Kevin, put him to bed and Jaehnel went to say, "Goodnight." He had his picture of him and Uncle Jeremy on his heart. Kevin said he didn't even see him take it off his dresser. I can't get over his connection with him.

Writing to Heal

MY FRIEND and I signed up for a hike called "Writing to Heal" sponsored by the Ridge and Valley Conservancy in our area. It was a beautiful day. We hiked, we stopped, we wrote, we had lunch, and we shared. A couple of days later, I was asked if I would write an article about it for the Ridge and Valley Newsletter, which would be about all the events sponsored by the Conservancy in 2018. I was happy to do it. I loved writing and it truly did help with healing. Here is what I submitted for the newsletter:

Writing to Heal: Letting Nature Take its Course

When a friend sent me the link to this event it spoke to me and I knew I had to sign up. The past year or so I am a changed person since I lost my beloved son. I trust that I am being guided to certain places, certain people and to do certain things. Reading and writing have become a huge part of my healing process, as has nature and the outdoors.

That's why I knew I was where I belonged when I met Margaret Schiller and seven other lovely ladies at the Limestone Ridge Preserve to begin a hike through the Ridge and Valley Conservancy Trails there. Margie encouraged us to listen to "our inner voice" as we ventured on her carefully and thoughtfully designed hike, including planned stops for inspired writing.

Our first stop was an area of rocky ledges with lots of moss growing on its edges. I wrote: "Life's rocky times; sharp and jagged but with hidden beauty, broken in different places with new life emerging."

Our next stop was a large tree that had fallen in a storm but had taken another large tree down with it. I wrote: "Life does not always end with old age—it can end with a disaster but every living thing leaves something beautiful behind. One life impacts so many others."

The next stop revealed another broken tree but so very different. Half of the tree was still standing vertically and the other half was perpendicular to it. Long splinters protruded out of each end of the tree as if the tree tried its hardest to hold together and not break. I wrote: "The tree splinters in many pieces when it breaks, not unlike the heart. The pieces hang on but the heart (and the tree) will never be whole again."

Next, we came upon a moving brook that we viewed from high above. To me, this is one of the most beautiful sounds of nature. I wrote: "Life is like a rippling brook. It flows on, touching all in its path, unending."

As we hiked along, we came to a rock wall built long ago. Margie offered her analogy and I thought it was perfect:

"Sometimes we build walls around us when we're in pain and, with time, the walls break down a bit."

We talked about the leaves changing and falling. Rather than thinking of them as dying I like to think of them as still living but in a different form.

We had an amazing lunch. We shared some of our writing. Even though I just met some of these ladies this day, we hugged. Nature has a way of opening your heart. This time I had the pleasure of great company in the woods but I am never really alone. My son Jeremy loved and appreciated the outdoors so much. I carry his spirit with me always.

So, I watch for lingering butterflies and birds. I look up and feel the warmth of the sun. I talk to the moon and the stars and look for rainbows. I plant and look forward to growth. Nature reminds me that the world is still a beautiful place and that life regenerates. We protect what we love. Let us encourage the world to love nature.

Messages From Heaven

October 25, 2018

WITH EXTREME GRIEF, there are bad days, worse days, and better days. In the beginning it is constant and after a while it comes in waves. I came home from watching Kolton for the day and Bob was in tears. He'd had a very bad day. "Missing my boy so much," he said. Sometimes the days that we have less distractions and aren't as busy are the worst because we spend a great deal of time thinking.

Bob told me that the lights in the house flashed on and off and he went in the bathroom and the towel had fallen off the rack.

I said, "Jeremy was trying to help you. I think he feels very sad when we are sad."

October 26, 2018

I picked up my grandson Josiah at the bus at 3:30. Jaehnel came over to pick him up about 4:10, as usual. We were sitting and talking when the alarm clock went off on my cell phone at 4:20. My alarm clock was not set for 4:20. I never get up that early. 4:20, the approximate time we assume of Jeremy's passing.

October 29, 2018
Jaehnel told me that Josiah woke up in the middle of the night with a fever. She went into his room and the ceiling fan was on. She asked Josiah if he turned it on and he said, "No, I can't even reach it." I think Jeremy was watching out for him.

October 31, 2018
We always go to the Halloween Parade in town and trick-or-treat for a while with our grandsons. Jaehnel told me that night when she put Kolty to bed he wanted to hold Jeremy's picture in his bed and said he misses him. He rubbed the picture on his cheek and said, "I love you, Jeremy." He does this on many nights, maybe it's when he feels Jeremy around. This tears at my heart.

November 11, 2018
My friend and I went to a one-woman play at a nearby college. It was called *Apples in Winter*. It was about a mom whose son has been in jail for twenty-two years on death row because he shot someone during a robbery for drugs. On this day, he will be put to death, and for his last meal has asked for his mother's apple pie. Since no food can be brought in from the outside, the jail has let the mom use their kitchen to bake the pie. She speaks her thoughts throughout the play while she bakes the pie. She doesn't know how this happened to her son. She shares the pain of fulfilling his last request. At the end she falls apart and slips to the floor in tears. She still loves her son and says goodbye. "You're the best." I got the chills when I heard those words, "You're the best."

November 13, 2018
It was the night before Jeremy's birthday and I was thinking about him. The lights browned out.

November 14, 2018
Jeremy's forty-first birthday; a birthday that he always said he would never make it to. Jaehnel and I were talking about what we should do for his birthday. She said she was thinking about Jeremy the night before and her lights browned out. She asked me if mine did too, and I said, "Yes." She said she had thought they probably did. Later that evening we let off biodegradable white balloons and wrote love messages on them.

November 30, 2018
We were gathered at my house for my friend's birthday. Jaehnel and her family were there. A song came on the radio by Creedence Clearwater Revival. Kolton said, "This is Jeremy's favorite song." Bob and Jaehnel both agreed that, "Yes, it is Jeremy's favorite song." It was a year and a half since Jeremy left us. Kolton was only two-and-a-half years old at the time. Could he actually be remembering all this or is Jeremy reminding him? A few months later, I listened to the lyrics of the song. Some of them were eerily speaking to me: *I see trouble on the way. It's bound to take your life. I know the end is coming soon.*

Ironically, I never knew this song was about death, but I can definitely see Jeremy relating to the lyrics, especially when he felt he wasn't going to live past forty years old.

December 4, 2018
I had to work, so Bob watched Kolton. The last couple of days Bob had said he didn't even feel like putting up a tree or decorations. I got home from work and Kolton said, "Momma,

wait till you see all the decorations." He was so excited and the house was completely decorated for Christmas. I looked at Bob and he said, "He was so excited that it got me excited." Then Kolton said, "Come see how we decorated Jeremy's room." There was a wreath and an electric candle in the window in the room that used to be Jeremy's. Oh, my heart.

December 6, 2018
I came home from a long day of training for work and there was a dime and a penny in the middle of my bed.

December 8, 2018
Bob went to Dennis's house to clean his gutters. Dennis has been a regular customer and Jeremy had worked there many times. Dennis and Jeremy were very fond of each other. When Bob was done with the gutters, he decided to blow all the leaves off the driveway for Dennis. This is something that Bob wouldn't normally do but Jeremy would. Bob said he just felt that something was telling him he should. In the middle of the driveway, Bob blew away the leaves to reveal a shiny dime and penny right next to each other in the middle of the driveway. I think Jeremy was proud of him.

December 9, 2018
It was the day of the Worldwide Candle Lighting for our children that have left this world too soon. Bob and I again attended the Candle Lighting Ceremony sponsored by the Compassionate Friends support group. Since it was a school night, Jaehnel decided to light the candles at home at 7:00 P.M. with Kevin and the boys. While Bob and I were lighting our candles at the ceremony, Jaehnel send me a text message that said, "We just lit our candles and the lights blinked three distinct times. Kevin and I looked at each other and cried."

December 13, 2018
Kolty wanted to hold the picture of him and Jeremy when he went to bed again. He said, "I want to see Jeremy for real. Do you know when my best day in the world was? I was in my crib and I heard footsteps and thought Momma was coming to get me and it was Jeremy!" I don't know if he was remembering something real or a dream.

December 15, 2018
It was Jaehnel's birthday. The year before I had given her a bracelet for her birthday. It had a little heart that contained a little bit of Jeremy's ashes. She was wearing the bracelet tonight. Kolton lightly kissed the bracelet and whispered, "Jeremy." Jaehnel looked surprised and said, "I never told him that the bracelet contained Jeremy's ashes!"

January 2, 2019
A new calendar year. New Year's was spent with Jaehnel, Kevin, and my grandsons. We ate, drank, played games, danced, and did karaoke. We stayed up for the New Year's ball drop. It made me realize how far I've come in one year. Last year I wanted to be in bed before twelve. I couldn't stand the whole idea of celebrating the past year or the upcoming year. There was nothing happy about it for me. This year I could at least participate in celebration. Even though Bob and I couldn't say "Happy New Year" to each other, we did say it to others.

I was getting dressed and thinking about how I had not had a sign from Jeremy for quite a while: over two weeks. Whenever that happens, I start to fear that the signs will stop and I won't feel his presence or his closeness anymore. My doctor says there are usually more signs the first year. Who knows why that is—maybe because they want to make sure their loved ones know they are okay and they want to know their loved ones are okay. Or maybe they cross over to another plane like some of the books say.

January 3, 2019
Kolton and I were grocery shopping and he asked if he could buy something from the candy stand near the check-out aisle. Of course, being the grandmother that I am, I said yes. He picked out gummy bears and said, "These are Jeremy's favorite and they are my favorite because Jeremy and I are buddies!" It's true, Jeremy loved gummy bears and they are buddies. Kolton never talks about Jeremy in the past tense, always in the present and I love it.

Later he was in Jeremy's bedroom and looked at a picture and said, "There's my buddy."

January 12, 2019
Jaehnel turned on the three electric candles she bought for the Candle Lighting Ceremony and went to put Kolton to bed. She came downstairs and two out of the three had turned off. She asked Kevin if he turned them off and he said no. She thought maybe their batteries had worn out but she picked them up and their switches were turned to the off position. Their batteries were not worn out at all.

January 13, 2019
Kolton was walking down the hallway on his way to bed and said, "You're the best, Jeremy." I just love the connection he has with Jeremy. The best thing is that he doesn't seem to find it scary or confusing. They say little ones usually lose this connection as they get older, but I truly hope that the light of love that connects them continues forever.

February 17, 2019

Kolty said to his mom, "Remember the night you went away in an ambulance and you didn't come back?"

"What do you mean?" she answered. "I've never been in an ambulance. Was it a dream, maybe?"

"No," he insisted. "I remember seeing you go away in it. It was the night you came home and kissed me on the head when I was in bed sleeping."

The night Jeremy died, Jaehnel was wailing with cries of pain and torment when I told her on the phone. She left her house to come to my house without going back inside to say good-bye to the boys. She didn't want them to see her that way. When she got home hours later, she went into each of the boys' bedrooms and kissed them on the head while they slept.

I believe Jeremy was telling Kolty that he was taken away in an ambulance and couldn't come back to say good-bye. He must have shown Kolty a vision of the ambulance. Kolty gets a look of confusion when he has these moments if people say they didn't happen. This child must be clairvoyant. I wonder if he will lose it as he gets older or embrace it. I so cherish the connection he has with Jeremy.

February 19, 2019

I was watching the boys at Jaehnel's house and Kolty said, "Tyler has a dog named Lucky, just like your cat Lucky. But Lucky isn't alive anymore."

"Yes, that's right," I said. "She's in heaven."

"Yes," Kolty said. "Remember Chubbs?"

"Chubbs," I said. "How do you remember Chubbs? You weren't even born."

He looked a little confused for a second and then said, "Josiah tells me about her."

Josiah said, "No I don't, I wasn't even born when Momma and Poppa had Chubbs."

Kolty still had that cute little face of confusion.

Chubbs was our beloved calico cat that we took in as a stray. Jeremy was quite an animal lover and when Chubbs, late in life, developed blindness and kidney failure he brought her to the vet and had her put to sleep. He brought her home and buried her in the back yard. I remember how upset he was that day. He was so sensitive and caring. I think maybe Jeremy was telling Kolty about Chubbs.

Spiritual Psychic Medium

I SAW ONLINE that Cathy McCall, Spiritual Psychic Medium, was going to be at one of the local yoga studios for "An Afternoon with Spirit." I had heard so many good things about Cathy that I immediately signed up. I shared the information, and two of my friends signed up as well.

Before my friend Joan picked me up, I went into what used to be Jeremy's bedroom and lay down on his bed. My dog, Grits, cuddled up next to me. I meditated for about fifteen minutes while listening to one of Deepak Chopra's meditations. I asked Jeremy to be there today at the Afternoon with Spirit. Then I got dressed, putting on my locket with Jeremy's picture and my bracelet with his Mother's Day card message to me engraved in his handwriting, and put his sobriety coin in my pocket and my pebble pal with Jeremy's name engraved on it in another pocket.

It was 2:00 in the afternoon as fifteen attendees waited for Cathy McCall to arrive at the studio. She emerged through the door as big as life with a warm smile and upbeat demeanor.

She personally introduced herself to each of us individually and shook our hands. She began by explaining what a psychic and a medium are. A psychic is capable of mental processes such as mental telepathy. A medium connects with people who have died and passed to the other side, the spiritual world, or as some call it, heaven. Cathy gets messages through all of her senses.

She said, "I see a couple, a man and a woman, a husband and wife. I can feel the man has passed from serious heart disease. He was a heavy smoker. I think the couple is Latin or Spanish, definitely from a different country. The woman is telling me that someone raised a child that wasn't theirs. Can anyone relate to this?"

I was the only one that raised my hand. I said, "Well, I don't know, I raised my niece because my sister was unable to and we are from a different country, but it's Germany, not a Spanish or Latin country. And my father died from heart disease and was a heavy smoker."

There is a younger male with them."

"My son," I said.

She continued, "Your mother wants to talk about this child you raised that she is the grandmother of. You had a lot of difficulty but you did well. You saved the day. Your father is not as vocal but he feels the same. There is a story around your mother's dysfunction." She asked, "Is there a sister that you have not spoken to in a very long time?"

I said, "Yes, the mother of my niece that I raised."

"Who is Robert?"

"My husband."

"Your son is coming through. When he was in the living world, he saw heartache. He passed through a rough time and didn't have the opportunity to say good-bye. There was much controversy surrounding his death. I feel it had something to do with addiction. Do you feel like you failed with this child?"

I said, "I just question if I did everything that I could."

"He says, 'You absolutely did everything.' He is sorry, sorry to all. He is well there and no longer has the issues he had here. He knows when you're holding his picture. Is there a song you listen to in the car? He says he sees you listening in the car?"

I said, "Yes, I went to an Alan Pederson concert. Alan Pederson is a father who lost his daughter several years ago and is an inspirational speaker, singer, and songwriter who travels around the country doing concerts for bereaved parents. I bought his CD and often listen to it in the car."

At one point, Cathy asked me if a certain male name meant anything to me. I will keep the name private. I said no because I was thinking that she was referring to someone that had already passed to the other side. It didn't hit me until later that it was the name of one of Jeremy's good friends. After Jeremy died, I wanted to know who gave or sold him the fentanyl that killed him. The friends he was with when he died pointed the finger at this young man; the name that Cathy said. I wonder if Jeremy was trying to tell me who it was.

Cathy said that Jeremy was telling her that if I hear noises in the house at night that it is him visiting. I told Cathy that I get signs from him all the time. She continued to sweep the room, bringing hope and peace to the guests that hoped to connect with their loved ones who had passed. At one point she said, "Someone wants to talk about German chocolate cake . . . or cupcakes. Is German chocolate cake a favorite of anyone's?" I couldn't believe it. I didn't say anything because I felt she had already spent a lot of time with me and there were fifteen other people in the room hoping for signs. But inside I was thinking about Valentine's Day. I made a batch of German chocolate cupcakes in the shape of hearts with pink icing. I said, "I'm just making cupcakes and cards for all of my loved ones, that's it. No gifts." I had always got Jeremy a chocolate heart or something for Valentine's Day. I think he wanted to thank me for the cupcakes and let me know he saw them.

Everyone in the room had a successful reading from Cathy, including the two friends I was with, Joan and JoVanah. JoVanah lost her son Dustin three months after Jeremy passed. She was sitting next to me holding Dustin's picture and Cathy said he kept trying to move in on my reading. She described Dustin perfectly and my friend JoVanah found some peace in her heart that day. If I didn't see it with my own eyes, I probably wouldn't believe it, but I did. What a magical mystery the spiritual world is!

Ask Him for Help

March 13, 2019

Bob recently returned from one of his many long weekend fishing trips. He had problems with his truck while he was up in New York State. He said he barely made it home. He began diagnosing what was wrong with the truck and found the CV joints needed replacing. Even though he's never done it before he was convinced he could manage the job. YouTube can teach you anything! He bought the parts and worked all day with frustration. He couldn't figure it out. He said he went in the garage to recharge and start over. He asked Jeremy for help. He said it came to him then, how the CV joints should go on. When he came in the house and told me this, I thought about the medium I went to see a year and a half ago who told me, "When you're stuck and need his help, ask Jeremy for it and he will help you."

March 14, 2019

My friend Antonette and I went up to Rochester, Vermont to attend When Words Count, a writing retreat. It truly was a retreat—a beautiful bed and breakfast type atmosphere in the Green Mountains. The owner and published author, Steve, generously helped us in the evenings with our writing. Amber, the Director of Culinary and Hospitality services, is an amazing chef and created the most delicious meals. There were seven ladies, all with a love of writing. We shared parts of our manuscripts with each other. We shared parts of our lives with each other. Even though we just met, we made connections. I believe that certain souls are meant to meet and be together.

March 21, 2019
Jaehnel told me she had a dream. She was crying to Jeremy and telling him she needed him to come back—that she would never be the same without him. He said, "It's okay," and hugged her. She said he looked good and he was happy. She said, "I really think it was him." I'm sure this dream was triggered by hearing that my sixty-two-year-old stepbrother Billy had tragically and suddenly suffered a massive heart attack. I have heard that when your loved ones appear healthy and perfect in your dreams, they are not just dreams but visits.

March 26, 2019
Today we said good-bye to my stepbrother Bill. The eulogies were beautiful tributes delivered by his mom, brother, uncle, daughter, and son. My stepbrother Walt said, "I'm not going to see Bill again." Both Bob and I told him to look for signs. "He is still here with you but in a different way." Walt is close to Bill, just as Jaehnel is close to her brother Jeremy.

A couple of days later I received an email from Walt. He said he went to work the previous day and they were testing the intercom system in his office. He first found it annoying but then realized that they were loudly playing the same songs that Bill used to play when they shared a two-family house. He used to get mad at Bill for blasting music. I smiled with tears streaming down my cheeks when I read it. I knew Bill would send signs.

April 5, 2019
Bob was working on our boat trailer, getting it ready for our vacation to South Carolina in a couple of weeks. Jeremy would have been right by his side. He loved working on mechanical projects with his dad. Bob went to the auto parts store to buy new bearings for the trailer. He was paying and looked down. There was a shiny penny right near the counter underneath him. Jeremy was right by his side.

April 6, 2019
I didn't sleep well. I was thinking about Jeremy all night long. April 6, 2017 was his last visit to his psychiatrist and the day we suspect he might have stopped taking his lithium. In the morning, Jaehnel sent me a text message. "I was thinking about Jeremy this morning as I was getting ready . . . I picked up my towel to dry my hair and a penny fell by my feet! I have no idea where it came from—it actually fell from my towel!!"

I later read in the online news that President Trump was applying pressure to Mexico to crack down on drugs there that are coming into our country. I also read that China was now cracking down on fentanyl entering the U.S. My first thought was, *It's about time*. I hope it's true and helps stop this tragic epidemic.

April 20, 2019
Bob and I arrived at our rented condo in Salem, South Carolina. We were exhausted after sixteen hours of driving. This was the first vacation we had taken with just the two of us since we lost Jeremy. All the other vacations were with friends or family. Unexpectedly, we both cried on and off the first day. We had no one there with us that we had to hold things together for. We simply let our tears flow. I had asked Jeremy to be with us and watch over us this week.

The condo complex was huge. I said we needed to go get a map so we headed to the clubhouse. Bob waited in the car while I went up the clubhouse steps. I heard music coming from inside and I recognized the song. Yep, it was none other than "Johnny B Good." Who would have thought that after not hearing this song for thirty years, we would hear it twice in less than two years?

The next day we put our boat in the lake. It was a beautiful day and we were fishing when the boat motor started to act up. We hoped we would make it back to the launch okay. Riding back, we noticed a butterfly circling our boat. It stayed with us, hovering around until we got back to the launch. Thanks Jeremy!

June 3, 2019

It was the third day after I brought my husband Bob for a medical test, a scope of his esophagus. He had been having difficulty swallowing, often choking on his food. He kept insisting it was allergies, but it kept getting worse until even he realized he should see a doctor. We were worried about the test but I was shocked when the doctor came out and said that there is a tumor that could be cancerous. We were to come to the office in a week when the biopsy results would be received and we could discuss the course of treatment. Bob, Jaehnel, and I all cried quietly on our own but we all decided we would fight this and beat it. We didn't tell anyone else anything yet.

I left the next day, June 4, to go to When Words Count Writing Retreat for six days. I was disappointed that I wouldn't be with my family on June 5, Jeremy's Angel Day. Jaehnel had been sick with a fever and cough so she stayed home from work this Monday to go to the doctor. She told me she wouldn't need me to pick up the boys at the bus stop today because she would be home to do it. Last minute she texted me and said she just got out of the doctor's office and had to get antibiotics, so could I pick up the boys? Yes, I could. I ran home to put my groceries away and went to the bus stop. My neighbor Jamie approached me at the bus stop. I often see her there as she has three little ones that either she or her husband pick up as well.

She said, "I have to tell you something and I hope you don't think I'm crazy. I didn't know whether to tell you. I called my mom and asked her if I should and she said yes, because she would want to know." I had no idea what she was talking about. "I had a dream last night. It was a vivid image of your son Jeremy. He said 'Please tell my Mom I love her and tell her to tell my family I love them. You have to tell her." Of course, I thanked Jamie for telling me and told her I believe in spiritual connections and have received many messages from Jeremy. She said, "I didn't understand why it would be me. I didn't know him that well, only from when he would pick up the boys at the bus stop."

I asked, "Has anything like this happened to you before?" She said there was one other time. Jeremy knew I would be seeing Jamie today and that she had the ability to receive his message. I thought about the last-minute change of plan for me to pick up the boys instead of their mom. If I didn't see Jamie today, I would never have received his message before I left for Vermont and before his Angel Day. He knew we needed extra love and prayers that week.

What Would They Say Now?

I have often wondered what Jeremy would say now if he could talk to me. I found two letters online that I thought would be quite accurate as to the thoughts of our lost children. I have shared them with my support group and would like to share them with you here:

A Letter From Heaven, by Lorelie Rozzano

Dear Mom and Dad,
Words can't begin to describe how sorry I am. I've put you in a position that no parent should ever face. I left—before you. It wasn't supposed to be this way. The natural order of things was skewed by my addiction. I can only imagine the agony you must be in. I know you're angry, despairing and sad, all at the same time. If only you could reach back in time and pluck me from the path I'd chosen, but you can't. You never could. God knows, you tried. I wasn't completely oblivious to all you did for me. I always believed I had time and the truth is—I was too damned smart for my own good.

I underestimated the power of my disease.

I know you tried to tell me this. But I wouldn't listen. When I began abusing drugs, I grew desensitized. I thought I was immortal. I liked living on the edge. I felt so alive! Drugs filled a place in me that nothing else could.

When I was high, I was King. When I was sober, I was just, well, me. Maybe that was part of the problem. I never did feel right, about being me. I always needed something more. I liked nice things. I wanted the best. I hated waiting for anything. When I wanted something, it was all I could think about until I got it, and then, I wanted something else. There were times I felt guilty for the stress I put you though. But it was fleeting. The burning need inside of me was greater than anything else. This need had no conscience, integrity, or morals.

There wasn't anything you could have said, or done, to prevent this from happening. I thought I knew it all. Death by overdose was something that happened to other people. Foolish people. People who didn't know shit about using. It wouldn't happen to me, no way, no how, not ever.

You begged me to stop. I tuned you out. Your words were like wasps in my ears. Although they stung, they were nothing more than an annoying buzz. When you cried, I cringed. When you put your arms around me, I wanted away from you. But there is no back. There is only forward. Please bring me forward.

Please don't blame yourself, or me. It will only make things worse. We did the best we could. You must believe this. If you don't we will all stay stuck and that would be a tragedy.

Take the love you have for me, and put it into the rest of our family. Every time you want to hug me, grab one of them. Then it will be like I'm part of the hug. Give us a great big squeeze and I promise, I'll feel it all the way up in heaven.

I hope you find peace in knowing I'm free in a way I never was before.

Up here, there is no addiction. There is only love. The kind of love that is greater than any of us will ever know below.

You might tell yourself that I am gone. But you're wrong. I'm right here. I'm the wind on your face, and the stars in the sky. I'm the raindrops, falling, outside your bedroom window. I'm the song of a bird, and the dawn of each new morning. I'm the clouds and the sun, and the waves in the ocean.

We will never part from one another. For love breathes life, even, in death. I am flesh of your flesh. Stand still—and you will feel me.

Love always, your child

I have often read this letter to myself and I can imagine Jeremy saying a lot of it. But Jeremy never called us names or stole from us. He also never felt "entitled to nice things." He wasn't materialistic and always worked hard to get the things he wanted. This letter helps me sometimes.

Here is another one that I found helpful and I hope it helps you too:

To the Family of an Addict Whose Addiction Won
by Christine Suhan

You did enough. I know you may not believe this now, but it's true.

The next few weeks will inevitably be filled with a relentless stream of questions. Should I have been more involved? Should I have been less involved? Should I have called him just one more time? Should I have left him in jail a little bit longer? Should I have hospitalized him? Should I have forced him into treatment? Should I have stopped enabling him? Should I have left him alone?

Truth be told, you might always feel like you could have done more to save your loved one. But please hear me when I tell you that you did enough. You did way more than enough. Loving him or her, despite their addiction, was the absolute best thing you could have done, and you did that so well. You loved them deeply. You saw past their pain and the ugly ways they ran from it, and you loved them anyway. Your love never failed and that will always be enough. Your love is the reason they kept fighting. And your love for them in this moment, and in every moment forward, is the reason they are resting peacefully.

You did everything right, even though it may feel like a lifetime of wrongs. So, when you're feeling at your weakest, immersed in the sadness of grief, please remember this:

It is not your Fault

You are likely drowning in a sea of guilt right now, but believe me when I say that nothing you did or didn't do caused your loved one to become an addict. I know it's hard to comprehend the baffling nature of the disease, but you did not cause this and despite your best efforts, you could not have prevented this. Addicts are born with a propensity toward becoming addicted. The addiction is triggered by a combination of many factors; elements over which you have little or no control. You are not at fault. You are not to blame.

I heard it said once that guilt is anger turned inward. Do yourself a favor and let the anger out. Direct it elsewhere. You are in no way responsible for the life he lived or the way he died.

It's OK to be Angry

You reserve the right to be angry. Losing a child (or a sister, mother, brother, father, friend) to the disease of addiction gives you a justifiable reason to be angry. But please don't be angry at them. Believe me, they didn't choose this life. They undoubtedly made several bad choices but they weren't in their right mind. The disease had warped reality so thoroughly that they weren't seeing the world as we see it. They were seeing a perception of reality that felt threatening, and their body and mind kicked into survival mode. And while trying to protect themselves, even though outwardly, it looked like self-destruction.

Be mad, but don't be mad at them. Be mad at the disease of addiction. Use that anger to fuel a passion for helping other addicts and their families find a way out. Your son or daughter (or friend or parent) did not choose to leave you—broken, hurting, and empty. They weren't the one choosing. And their disease didn't care about you or even them. Get angry at the disease. Seek revenge on his or her behalf by spreading awareness, hope, and shedding light on the realities of addiction. The worst thing you could do right now would be to stay silent because silence feeds the disease.

Your Story is Worth Telling

Addiction is a family disease. Although you might feel as if this is not your story to tell, I assure you that you are as much a part of the story as the addict. You were in it together. As much as your loved one tried to shut you out, you were still in it with them. You were probably more emotionally affected by their addiction than they were. Addicts often begin using drugs and alcohol as a way to numb their feelings and they continue using because it works. For a while, the drugs effectively numb the pain. But you didn't have a numbing agent to turn to while your family was walking through hell. You felt the gravity of the situation. You carried the weight of his addiction. You were the one who was thinking and feeling clearly and you have a powerful story to tell.

Shame might try and stop you from telling you story. It might tell you your story isn't worth telling because the disease won, but listen closely: Your story can and will save lives. Owning and sharing your experience is the bravest way to fight the disease. The life of your loved one mattered, and their death has the potential to matter even more. Help to make his or her story—your story—matter.

Don't Shut People Out

Despite the overwhelming presence of addiction and the rapid rise in suicide and accidental overdoses, people are extremely uncomfortable talking about addiction. Your friends don't know how to navigate this painful time. If they are shying away, that doesn't mean they don't care. They are just lost. They don't know what to say or what to do; they need your guidance. You might not even know what you need right now, but when you start to figure it out, tell them. Let your people in. Show them how to support you. If you want to talk about him, tell them that. If you want to talk about his death or his disease, talk to them. Your friends want to be there for you, they just don't know how.

You will get through this, and the acute pain you feel right now will lessen. Their death will inevitably change you, but it doesn't have to destroy you. Let the grief evolve you. Let your love for them propel you into a dimension of living you never knew was possible. But in the meantime, rest assured that the hearts of other families rocked by addiction are bleeding with you.

With Love,
A recovering addict,
whose demons are the same
as your loved one's
(Christine Suhan 2020)

The Gift of Hope

I ALREADY KNOW the last contribution that I will make to this cause. The Harvard Psychiatry Brain Collection collects brain tissue from families with serious brain disorders. The brain tissue is used for scientific investigations of the underlying causes of neuropsychiatric brain disorders. They collect tissue from:

1) Individuals with a psychiatric diagnosis (schizophrenia, manic-depression, obsessive-compulsive disorder),

2) First-degree relatives (parents, siblings, offspring) of individuals with a psychiatric diagnosis, and

3) "Normal control" individuals who have no family history of mental illness.

Individuals interested in donating their brain can preregister or the decision can be made by surviving family at the time of death. (800) BRAIN BA (272-4622)

My Reasons

For Me

My reasons for writing this book are many. Some are for myself and some are for others. Firstly, writing is so therapeutic and has been a big part of my healing process. I am an overthinker. Thoughts and ideas are constantly overcrowding my brain. I would imagine this is a common trait for people that like to write. When I write these ideas down, I don't have to worry so much about keeping them in my mind. I don't want to forget them. It is a way for me to release a little more of my pain each time I write things down.

My thoughts and ideas become more aligned and organized if I write them down. I didn't know that I was going to write a book when I started journaling all my thoughts, but I referred to my notes and journal often while writing this book.

For My Family

I want all those who knew Jeremy to continue to know and remember him. I want my grandchildren not to forget him and I want their children to know him as well. I also want future generations to know the history of our family for medical and heritage reasons.

For Other Bereaved Parents

Another reason I wrote this book was for other bereaved parents. I have developed so much compassion for the bereaved parent. I have lost both of my parents and several friends but the depth of grief I have felt in losing my son is indescribable. There is no greater pain.

My son was an adult when he died. I have met many parents who have lost their children so much younger and think how they would probably be grateful if their child was able to live to the age of thirty-nine like Jeremy did. But for me there is still that void, that pain and those thoughts that he is still supposed to be here.

I also have a daughter and grandchildren. At some point after Jeremy's death, they helped me want to go on. I remember when my mother took her own life and I thought she didn't love me enough to stay. This created a lot of anxiety for me as a child and affected my self-esteem. If I bury myself in my grief, will my daughter and grandsons think that I didn't love them enough to go on? I still have so much to share with them.

If you have other children and grandchildren, remember you are still fortunate to have them and that is a great reason to try to come out of this grief journey as the best version of yourself that you can be. Don't let your other children feel like the forgotten siblings. They are grieving, too. I have met many parents in my support groups who don't have other children or grandchildren. Some have even lost two children. I can't imagine twice the pain that I have endured and I have all the more compassion for them.

By no means am I telling you to push yourself or try to rush through grief. I believe quite the opposite. I broke down and cried for some part of every day for over a year. Tears are healing and relieve some of the pain. Do what you need to do. Cry, sleep, spend time alone if you need to.

Once you decide to try to go out to a social function, don't feel bad if you don't feel up to it when the time comes, or if you have to leave early. You can even tell your host that you want to try to come but you don't know what kind of day you will be having or that you might have to leave early. Go at your own pace.

If you have other children, you might need help. Don't be afraid to ask friends or family for help. Most people want to help but don't know what to do and they are grateful to know what they can do to help.

Everyone's grief journey is different, but I have found it helpful for bereaved parents to share what has been helpful for them with other bereaved parents. Sometimes it helps and sometimes it doesn't.

For example, I have had three different parents whose children passed tell me at different times that there is a certain sense of relief in the loss. One parent's son had bipolar and died by suicide. She had another family member who had bipolar and he and the family experienced a tragic struggle. She was relieved that she didn't have to go through it again. When she told her husband how she felt, it caused a divorce. Two other parents, one of a teen and one of a young adult, shared with me that they didn't have to stay up late worrying anymore. "At least now we know where they are and that they are safe."

I could not relate to this outlook at all. We went through terribly stressful times with Jeremy's illness, but I would take back all the worrying and all the sleepless nights waiting for the phone to ring. I would take all that back to have him here with me still. I know this was probably meant to be a comfort, but it wasn't to me. Sometimes people will say the wrong things but we need to remember their intent is to help.

Most of what has helped me has already been mentioned, but I just want to highlight and clarify some of the things most beneficial. If you are a bereaved parent reading this book, you already know that reading books has been as helpful to me as writing. As I have said, I read books about the afterlife and grief but I also read books that are specific to my situation, such as books about bipolar disorder, mental illness, substance use disorder, suicide, and the opioid epidemic. You may find it helpful to read and learn through books more specific to your situation.

Another thing that has been extremely helpful is my support groups. I now belong to three support groups: the Compassionate Friends, which is a group for parents who lost their children at any age and for any reason, and the other two groups are for parents whose children were lost to drugs or alcohol. There is something to be said for connecting with other parents whose children died under similar circumstances. Even in the Compassionate Friends, it seems that we are drawn to the people who have had more similar experiences.

My husband came to the first few Compassionate Friends meetings with me, but he stopped going, which is fine because what is helpful for me might not be helpful for him or for someone else. Many people think it is too sad and will keep you sad. For me it is a place that is safe for me and other parents. There is a kind and silent understanding among bereaved parents. I know I can say anything and I can cry if I need to. I know I won't be judged. I will be comforted and supported as I try to comfort and support others. Helping is healing.

Music has been helpful in my grief journey. If you love music, it will help you, too. I find certain songs are meaningful and inspiring.

If you can find it in your spiritual or religious belief to believe in the afterlife, this is probably what has helped me the most. Just knowing that Jeremy is here with me has led me to a spiritual enlightenment like no other. Open your heart and your mind and look for signs. I never knew that there was so much proof and scientific connection to the afterlife. Being around so many bereaved parents, I realize that the questioning of faith and spiritual beliefs is very normal.

It surprised me how so many bereaved parents have had undeniable signs from their children. All of this just gives more validation to it. You need to decide how or if it fits into your beliefs, but I hope it does. I believe that I will be with Jeremy again someday but I know I still have a purpose here on earth.

You may want to see a medium, but be careful. There are many mediums with a gift but there are also many that are frauds. If you decide to go, make sure it is someone highly recommended with a record of success.

Surround yourself with people that you are comfortable being around. I am usually a person who takes a long time to get close to a person. However, over the past year I have made more than a dozen new friends who I feel closer to than some friends that I've known for years. We have that common bond, the common thread that other friendships lack. We wish that we became connected for a different reason, but we are glad we are connected.

One of my friends, who I have known for years, has recently ended our friendship. I don't think she approved of how openly I was handling my grief. I am fortunate that my other friends and family were very supportive. They dropped everything in their lives on a moment's notice and rushed to our side. When I started to go out, they rallied around me, always watching out for us, making sure that we were okay.

Your grief journey will last a lifetime. You will carry the ache with you forever. But once you get used to the pain, you will become more functional and learn coping methods. You will never be the same person. You will be a transformed person. If you are married, your spouse will be a transformed person as well. Many marriages do not survive when they lose a child. Both people in the couple change and their changes may not correspond with each other anymore.

Our marriage has survived, but there was a time in the beginning when we both wondered whether it would. We have both respected each other's way of grieving, and in the end, have learned that there is no place for blame in our marriage. No one else understands us like we do each other. We have both lost the same beautiful boy, have experienced the same beautiful joy, memories, and laughter he has brought us. Most of all, we have both experienced the pain.

Bob relieves his pain by fishing. He spends so much time fishing, and the more time he spends fishing, the happier it makes me because I know the pain and I know how important it is to find things that are healing. Fishing is a part of his self-care. We both have experienced the same loss, but how we process our grief is very different.

Being in nature is also very healing for me. Belief in the afterlife and being in nature goes without saying because there are so many signs in nature. Since Jeremy loved the outdoors as much as we do, it makes sense that many of his signs come through nature. To me, nature is my true church—God's creation. For me, God is the universe, in all things loving and beautiful.

After our poor cat was killed by the bobcat in 2018, our house was pet-less for the first time ever. I knew that if Jeremy was here, he would want us to get another pet. He loved animals so much.

I was inspired that a dog would provide therapeutic value for me since back in April, 2018, when I had brought my friend Antonette to the hospital for a surgical procedure. I was there for ten hours through the preparation, surgery, and recovery time. I had brought plenty of things to read in the waiting area. At one point, someone brought in a therapy dogs and brought it over to meet me. It was a gentle black lab. When the dog left, I looked at all the pictures of the therapy dogs on the poster boards. I thought, maybe that's what I needed, a therapy dog. We hadn't had a dog for a number of years because our cat did not get along with dogs and would hide in a room sometimes for days if one came to visit.

I started skimming through the rescue sights online and going to a few dog adoption days but couldn't find just the right dog. I didn't want a dog too big, and it had to be a dog that was good with kids because my grandchildren are over all the time. One day I came across an almost all-white puppy with tan ears and patches. He was part beagle and part terrier and they really weren't sure what the father was. We met the puppy and he was so cute and sweet we took him home that day. He was four-and-a-half months old, and we named him Grits. Right away he wanted to sleep with me and would crawl up and lay down right next to my heart. I think dogs can sense when you are hurting.

During my grief journey, I decided to take a meditation class at a Buddhist monastery, Bodhi Monastery. I had read that meditation can help you stay grounded emotionally and can help you be spiritually connected. A Buddhist monk taught the class. He explained that it takes practice—keep practicing and all of a sudden you will get it. I started out using guided imagery, imagining a beautiful place, quiet and calm. I usually imagined a beach, mountain, or garden view. After a while I stopped using imagery because I noticed that when I was meditating with my eyes closed, I would start to see visions. Usually they were visions of Jeremy, with his facial features unbelievably detailed. Sometimes there were faces of other people, like Jaehnel or Bob, sometimes even my dog, but most of the time it was pictures of Jeremy—some of a younger Jeremy, but most more recent.

In the beginning of a grief journey, you need help. You are probably not strong enough to reach out to help someone else. About nine months into my grief, I felt that I wanted to become involved in advocacy. I was already a volunteer for American Foundation for Suicide Prevention and participated annually in their Out of the Darkness Walk in honor of my mother, as well as my half-sister and now also my son. The American Foundation for Suicide Prevention does a lot for mental health research and awareness because most people who die by suicide or who attempt suicide are suffering from a mental illness.

I joined our County National Council for Alcohol and Drug Dependence (NCADD). I participated in two 5K walks for addiction and recovery. When our local area started their own coalition, the Blairstown CARE Coalition, I started to attend and become involved in that. All communities are suffering from this problem. We can't save the whole world, so why not start in our own community? I was so pleased to join this group of compassionate citizens, law enforcement, and educators who were driven to make a difference in their community.

We are working on important pursuits such as putting prevention programs in the local high school, a local support group, awareness campaigns, and more. I do feel that there should be a mandated class in high school in 11th or 12th grade about mental illnesses, including early signs and symptoms of anxiety, depression, substance use disorder, bipolar, and PTSD, and available treatments for them. I think it would be a great topic for teachers' in-service days and parents' meetings. Jeremy was seventeen when his symptoms reached the criteria for diagnosis. He, his friends, his teachers, and the vice principal did not understand what was going on. We, as a family, had to teach ourselves about bipolar. We had a bit of a jump start because of our family history; this was not our first experience with it. Each family that is prepared and knowledgeable increases the chances of a better outcome.

I recently applied and was accepted to be a recovery coach for the Community Law Enforcement Addiction Recovery Program (CLEAR). Our county law enforcement and our Center for Prevention & Counseling have partnered for this new innovative program. Anyone can go into the police department or the Center and ask for help with addiction without being arrested. Recovery coaches are called in to police stations and hospital emergency rooms to help the individual or their family members connect with treatment and services. I also continued my classes to complete the Certified Peer Recovery Specialist program. I learned so much. A lot of which I wish I knew earlier in my life. Marijuana is so much stronger today than it was years ago. My mind goes back to Jeremy's first psychiatrist who told us how much marijuana can aggravate an already predisposed mental illness. Research has shown a direct correlation between marijuana, psychosis and mental illness. The teen brain can especially be affected. When considering legalization of recreational marijuana, concern should be given to the message we're sending to our youth. Brains are not fully developed until the age of 26. Areas that have legalized adult recreational marijuana have shown increases in adolescent marijuana use. The age of onset of a mental illness is often between 16-26 but the age of the onset of marijuana use is often younger than that. We often don't know yet which youth are more vulnerable to addiction and mental illness.

(Luke Niforatos 2020)

I also learned how there is not one type of treatment that is successful for everyone. Some individuals get better and some go through a lifetime of rehabs without ever reaching recovery.

With the opioid epidemic and the increasing fentanyl in the drug supply reaching extreme proportions, medication assisted treatment (methadone, buprenophine and naltrexone, has been at an all-time need to save lives. Many treatment facilities have not caught up with the epidemic and are running rehabs traditionally as they did years ago. (Jeffrey Foote, PhD, Carrie Wilkens, PhD, Nicole Kosanke, PhD Stephanie Higgs 2014)

Above all, we need to always remember that substance use disorder is not a moral weakness. It is a disease with a biological basis. The structure of the brain is changed and damaged and can stay that way for a long time even after abstaining from use. That's why relapse is very common.

The most important reason for writing this book is to help bring change. I hope people will be left with less stigma, better understanding and greater awareness of mental illness, substance use disorders, suicide, the opioid epidemic and the dangers of fentanyl poisoning during present times.

Here and Now

AFTER JEREMY'S PASSING, so many people who knew and loved him told me how Jeremy left an impact on everyone he knew. This is true, but there is no reason he has to stop leaving an impact. I know it is my purpose to continue his impact on the world. He is here with me and we are doing this together. I truly feel and believe that I am being guided from the other side through every open door that comes my way, so I will follow my path. When you feel you are strong enough to move forward, take your loved one with you.

I want to summarize and leave a reference list of all the things that have helped me because I love lists. They make me feel organized. Remember, everyone grieves differently, but if you are a bereaved parent you might find something that will help you as well:

- Cry, sleep, be with people, be alone—whatever you need to do—in your own time
- Writing/journaling
- Reading books

- Support groups
- Gratitude
- Music
- Being in nature
- Faith in the afterlife
- A group or private visit to a medium/psychic
- See a grief counselor
- Meditation
- Surround yourself with the right people
- Save a life: adopt a pet
- Plant a garden in honor of your child
- Do things in your child's memory/name
- Advocacy
- Volunteer

Remember, there is no timeline—each parent has to find what helps them, but only when they are ready.

You may find it hard to believe that Gratitude is on the list. But there are gifts that come from grief even though it may take a long time to see them. Of course, it goes without saying that I would give all those gifts back to have my son back again and to have been able to change the course of the lives of my half-sister and mother.

I am grateful that even though Jeremy had his struggles in life, I don't think he suffered in death. I am grateful for my husband, daughter, grandchildren, and all my other loved family and friends. I am grateful for my new friends who I have gained through support groups and advocacy groups. My life is richer with them in it.

I am thankful for every person who cared so much about Jeremy and us and reached out to us. They continue to be a support for us. I am fortunate to have had such a spiritual awakening and to continue to have Jeremy's spirit with me always. I know many bereaved parents who have not noticed signs from their children and it is something that has helped me so much. I have grieved so much and will always grieve my losses, but I realize that the more love there is, the more grief there is, and there is more of a connection with your loved one.

I am so grateful to have had Jeremy, even though his life was cut short. When he was happy, he was so happy. He had such a sense of humor and always kept us laughing. He was so loving towards people and animals and was loved by so many. He was never jealous or malicious. He was a beautiful baby and child and such a handsome adult. I am grateful to have spent thirty-nine years with him rather than never to have known him.

I have had so much opportunity to advocate for and honor Jeremy. I can feel him cheering me on. I believe I have been guided to see my purpose and maybe Jeremy's, Ruth's, and my mother's purposes. I live not only for me, but them as well. I hope that some of what I do will change the world in some small way for the better and become a living tribute to Jeremy's life. Then he will never be entirely gone.

If I can positively impact one life and everyone reading this book impacts a life, hopefully that will be a lot of lives spared. We can accomplish more together than we can alone. I truly feel that if we can improve or find solutions to one of these problems, it will have a positive effect on the others. As you know now, several of these issues have profoundly affected my family, but they all affect our world and are constantly causing loss of life. Let us all help there be less grieving in the world.

I wish I had true solutions to these problems but knowledge, awareness, and advocacy is a great place to begin.

Every person whose life my son touches is part of his legacy. I will continue his legacy for as long as I am here. Searching for him is all-encompassing. I long for his presence in any way I can see, hear, smell, or feel him or be his voice.

I can't really say it gets easier but I do get stronger. Telling my story makes my inner soul and my heart a little stronger each time. Thanks to my readers, for joining me on this journey.

Acknowledgments

I AM GRATEFUL to many who helped me on this journey. First, this book would have never been written if Steve Eisner from the When Words Count Writing Retreat didn't talk me into writing it and I'm so glad he did. Of course, the retreat led me to my circle of writing sisters who cried with me, held me, and encouraged me to keep going. Gratitude also goes to my publisher Dede Cummings, of Green Writers Press, who saw the value of my words and understood my purpose. Also, my editors Peggy Moran, Rose Alexandre-Leach, and Ferne Johansson who helped me make my book better.

The members of my family were the first readers and gave me their blessing to reveal our family story, which I know was a difficult decision. I am forever beholden to Christa, Elissa, Jaehnel, Marilyn, and my husband Bob for their encouragement and their understanding my need to tell our story. It is also their story.

Lastly, but most important, I need to mention my inspiration: my mother, Alma Jaehnel, my half-sister, Ruth Klancke, and my son, Jeremy, who had to struggle through the darkness. Mostly to my son Jeremy, who stayed by my side the whole time I was writing, putting the words in my heart as I wrote them down—we did this together. Forever connected. Love never dies.

References

Addiction Policy Forum, "What is Addiction?" www.addictionpolicy.org, 2019)

Duffy, Ann, M.D.,2019, *Brain and Behavior Research Annual Report*)

Foote, Jeffrey PhD, Carrie Wilkens, PHD, Nicole Kosanke, PHD Stephanie Higgs, 2014, *Beyond Addiction,* Simon and Schuster, New York, NY

Macy, Beth 2018, *Dopesick, Dealers, Doctors, and the Drug Company that Addicted America*, Brown and Company, 2018)

Niforatos, Luke, 2020 *Marijuana Impact Symposium,* SAM(Smart Approaches to Marijuana)

Rowell, Victoria 2018, *The Women Who Raised Me, A Memoir,* William Morrow Publishing, New York, N.Y.

Rozzano, Lorelie 2016, A Letter From Heaven, www.jaggedlittleedges.com.

Smith Judie 1986, *Coping with Suicide*, The Rosen Publishing Group, New York, New York)

Suhan, Christine 2020 "To the Family of an Addict Whose Addiction Won," www.filterfreeparents.com,

Web MD, www.webmd.com/bipolar-disorder/mental-health, accessed January 2018)

Westoff Ben 2019, *Fentanyl, Inc., How Rogue Chemists Are Creating the Deadliest Wave of the Opioid Epidemic*, Blackstone Publishing.

Resources

American Foundation for Suicide Prevention:
www.afsp.org

Brain and Behavior Research Foundation
www.bbrfoundation.org

Compassionate Friends
(bereaved parents, grandparents, siblings)
www.compassionatefriends.org

National Alliance on Mental Illness
www.nami.org

National Institute on Drug Abuse
www.drugabuse.gov

Smart Approaches to Marijuana
www.learnaboutsam.org

Lost Voices of Fentanyl
www.lvof.org

Fentanyl Awareness Coalition
www.the-fac.org

Bibliography

Alexander, Eben. *Proof of Heaven: A Neurosurgeon's Journey into the Afterlife.* New York: Simon & Schuster, 2012.

Amatuzio Janis. *Beyond Knowing: Mysteries and Messages of Death and Life from a Forensic Pathologist.* New York: New World Library, 2006.

Amatuzio. *Forever Ours: Real Stories of Immortality and Living from a Forensic Pathologist. Novato, California*: New World Library, 2007.

Bernstein J. *When The Bough Breaks: Forever After the Death of a Son or Daughter.* Kansas: Andrews McMeel Pub., 1997.

Beth, Macy. *Dopesick: Dealers, Doctors, and the Drug Company that Addicted America.* New York: Little, Brown and Company, 2018.

Brown, Charita Cole. *Defying the Verdict, My Bipolar Life.* Chicago: Curbside Splendor Publishing, 2018.

DuBois, Allison. *Don't Kiss Them Goodbye.* New York: Fireside, 2005.

Duke, Patty. *A Brilliant Madness Living With Manic-Depressive Illness.* New York: Bantam, 1992.

Foote, Wilkens, Kosanke & Higgs. *Beyond Addiction: How Science and Kindness Help People Change.* New York: Scribner, 2014.

James & Friedman. *The Grief Recovery Handbook: The Action Program for Moving Beyond Death, Divorce, and Other Losses including Health, Career, and Faith.* Colorado: Collins Living, 2009.

Kagan, Annie. *The Afterlife of Billy Fingers: How My Bad-Boy Brother Proved to Me There's Life After Death.* Newburyport: Hampton Roads Publishing, 2013.

Kaiser, Karen, PhD. *Born into Madness: When Those Who Are Supposed to Love You Can't.* Leesburg, VA: Karen R. Kaiser, Ph.D., 2020.

Mitchel, Kathleen. *Treasures in Tragedy: A Mom Finds Hope in Grief and Loss.* Denver: Treasured Bookworks, 2020.

Powers, Ron. *No One Cares About Crazy People: The Chaos and Heartbreak of Mental Health in America.* New York: Hachette Books, 2017.

Ragan, Lyn. *Signs from the Afterlife: Identifying Gifts From The Other Side.* Atlanta: Lyn Ragan, 2014.

Rozzano, Lorelie. *Jagged Little Edges.* Canada: Lorelie Rozzano, 2013.

Rowell, Victoria. *The Women Who Raised Me.* New York: William Morrow, 2008

Smith, Judie. *Coping With Suicide: A Resource Book for Teenagers and Young Adults.* New York: Rosen Pub Group, 1989.

Westoff, Ben. *Fentanyl, Inc.: How Rogue Chemists Are Creating the Deadliest Wave of the Opioid Epidemic* Washington: Atlantic Monthly Press, 2019.

Endnotes

Page

24 *Coping with Suicide*, Judie Smith, 1986

59 www.WebMD - "Bipolar Disorder/Mental Health"

75 www.addictionpolicyforum, "What is Addiction"?

99 *Fentanyl Inc.*, Ben Westoff, 2019

99 www.drugfreenj.org, "Knock Out Opiate Abuse," *Drug Monitoring Iniative*, 2020

111 *Dopesick*, Beth Macy 2018

154 *Brain and Behavior Research Annual Report,* Ann Duffy, MD, 2019

About the Author

RENATE LEDUC has a B.S. in Education and Psychology from East Stroudsburg University. She retired from the Social Work field where she was with Child Protective Services. Renate was a substitute teacher and facilitator for Child Assault Prevention in the schools. She currently volunteers as a Field Advocate for AFSP (American Foundation for Suicide Prevention) and as a Certified Peer Recovery Specialist. She is also involved in advocacy for Mental Health, Suicide, Addiction, and Fentanyl Awareness. She hopes to help others by telling her story.